A SPY IN THEIR MIDST

A SPY IN THEIR MIDST

The World War II Struggle of a Japanese-American Hero

The story of
Richard Sakakida
as told to
Wayne Kiyosaki

Madison Books
Lanham • New York • London

Published by Madison Books
4720 Boston Way
Lanham, Maryland 20706

3 Henrietta Street
London WC2E 8LU England

Distributed by National Book Network

The paper used in this publication meets the minimum requirements of American
National Standard for Information Sciences—Permanence of Paper for Printed
Library Materials, ANSI Z39.48—1984. ∞ ™

Manufactured in the United States of America.

Library of Congress Cataloging-in-Publication Data

Kiyosaki, Wayne S., 1931–
A spy in their midst : the World War II struggle of a Japanese-
American hero / Wayne S. Kiyosaki.
p. cm.
Includes bibliographical references and index.
1. Sakakida, Richard. 2. World War, 1939–1945—Participation,
Japanese American. 3. World War, 1939–1945—Secret service—United
States. 4. World War, 1939–1945—Military intelligence—
Philippines. 5. Prisoners of war—Japan—Biography. 6. Prisoners
of war—United States—Biography. 7. World war, 1939–1945—Prisons
and prisoners, Japanese. I. Title.
D810.S8S345 1995 940.54'04—dc20 94-46954 CIP

ISBN 1-56833-044-8

To the members of the
Corps of Intelligence Police, Manila Detachment
G2, Headquarters Philippine Department,
U.S. Army

CONTENTS

FOREWORD

The story of Richard Sakakida, a second-generation Japanese-American from Hawaii who served as a U.S. Army undercover agent in the Philippines during the Second World War, is a remarkable tale of courage, daring, and sacrifice. It is an account of how one man, working in virtual isolation, endured torture, privation, and the perpetual threat of discovery to undertake vital intelligence operations in the heart of Japanese Army headquarters.

In contrast to his Japanese-American brethren who faced German troops in Europe as part of the fabled 100th Infantry Battalion/442d Regimental Combat Team, Sakakida confronted in the Philippines an enemy of his own race and ancestry. In this respect, his experience is similar to that of the six thousand *nisei* constituting the Military Intelligence Service (MIS) who provided language-based intelligence support to combat units in the Pacific theater. However, unlike members of either the 100th/442d or MIS, Sakakida fought the Japanese from within their own ranks, not across battlefield lines. Thus, Sakakida's experience is altogether unique.

Though much has been written about Sakakida since his story was first made public at a veterans' reunion in 1991, the work that follows is the most detailed and accurate account to date of his war-time service. Moreover, it delves deeply into the historic forces and cultural and social values that formed young Sakakida's character in prewar Hawaii, forces and values that shaped his response to the challenge he encountered as a soldier-spy.

This book constitutes an important addition to the literature of World War II. I hope that it will generate interest in, and appreciation for, the significant, but little known contributions of Japanese-Americans to the Allied victory. Indeed, this absorbing work perfectly illustrates the truism that the strength of the nation lies in diversity—that patriotism is a state of mind, not an accident of birth.

In the end, this story is about individual courage and how pride and endurance can overcome seemingly insurmountable obstacles. Like any tale of derring-do, it reflects what we honor in our heroes. In this day of the antihero, which celebrates people's failings rather than their achievements, we need examples like Richard Sakakida to redefine our self-imposed limitations and inspire us to greater deeds.

Daniel K. Akaka
U.S. Senator
Democrat-Hawaii

PREFACE

Secrecy is part of the craft of intelligence. Because of that, for nearly fifty years official accounts of Richard Sakakida's mission to the Philippines as a U.S. undercover agent were confined to the classified archives of the United States Army.

In 1987, the U.S. Army Intelligence and Security Command featured his story in a book entitled *Military Intelligence: Its Heroes and Legends*. In 1991, Sakakida himself delivered a poignant account of his experience as the guest speaker at the fiftieth anniversary observance of the U.S. Military Intelligence Service, held in Monterey, California. Sakakida's speech enthralled his listeners and led, ultimately, to my decision to write this book.

Richard agreed to meet with me and generously gave his time to a number of lengthy conversations. In these pages I have focused on events during the period of 1941 to 1945, but I have also woven in experiences from his other years of service that enrich this remarkable story.

It became obvious to me as I listened to Richard talk that his experience between 1941 and 1945 was significantly influenced by his upbringing. Thus, some discussion of his formative years is pro-

11

vided to shed light on the underlying cultural influences that he felt during his lonely pursuit of a precarious mission. His survival as a prisoner of war of the Japanese occupation force in the Philippines is an important testimony to the importance of culture in shaping a person's character.

Sakakida's story is unique in many respects. Most unusual of all is the fact that he was the only American intelligence agent of Japanese ancestry to be held in captivity by the Japanese. In all of World War II, only two Japanese-Americans were captured by the Japanese side. The other was Frank Fujita, a member of an artillery unit from Texas, who was captured in Java.

Before his capture, the terrifying personal consequences that Sakakida might suffer at the hands of the enemy was a concern of the American military command in the Philippines. They ordered him to depart before the American surrender, but he volunteered to remain behind. The reason for his decision is part of this story. Suffice it to say that his situation, as he awaited capture, was fraught with terrifying implications because of his Japanese ancestry.

The year 1942 was not good for Japanese-Americans in either America or Japan. In the hysteria that followed the Japanese attack on Pearl Harbor, even some of the most liberal thinkers in America supported the U.S. government decision to herd Japanese-Americans into what were essentially concentration camps. Thus, the threat of becoming prisoners of war was as real on the American side as it was on the side of the enemy.

Ironically, once he became a POW, some of his Japanese captors were inclined to see Sakakida as a traitor even though Japanese-Americans were regarded as no more than *gaijin*, or foreigners, under normal circumstances.

Sakakida's story also magnifies the improbability of achieving a consistent definition of what has popularly been trumpeted as "internationalization" whenever national interests have come into conflict between the United States and Japan. It is a reminder of the importance of enlightened diplomacy in heading off armed conflicts. Whenever serious disagreements have arisen between the United States and Japan, the Japanese-Americans and other Asian-Americans who have had the misfortune to be mistakenly identified as

Japanese have borne the onus of scapegoats. The reason is that they are "different," an idea familiar to some Japan specialists today who call for measures against Japan because it is different.

There is another bit of irony to this story. A cardinal principle embodied in the thoughts of the great Chinese military strategist Sun Tzu is that in war, one must know oneself as well as the enemy. Sakakida probably survived unspeakable mental and physical torture because he understood his captors as well as himself. Simply put, it took a Japanese frame of mind to survive Japanese methods of punishment. As a young man, Sakakida almost entered the Buddhist priesthood, the education for which would have entailed long years of ascetic training in physical and mental endurance. In many respects, he understood the transcendental aspects of mind and body better than some of his tormentors in prison.

In order to understand the extraordinary willpower of Sakakida and the men of the legendary Japanese-American 100th Infantry Battalion and 442d Regimental Combat Team, and the Military Intelligence Service (MIS) as American soldiers, one must take into account a rather unique process of Americanization that was occurring in Hawaii.

The process was led by the first generation of Japanese immigrants whose only hope for a stake in American life lay with their American-born children. They were mostly laborers, poor and lacking in much formal education. They were philosophical about the harsh realities of life without even knowing what philosophy was about. But they brought to the islands a compelling work ethic and fierce pride in their cultural, ehtical, and historical heritage.

They had learned from Buddhism to accept fate, from Confucianism the importance of filial piety and loyalty, and from Shintoism an abiding faith in the transcendental quality of nature. Thus, being poor was not bad; it was the starting point for hope. Personal and material aggrandizement were discouraged in favor of family and group needs, and the gifts of nature were revered and cultivated so that gardens filled with flowers and greenery could stay the ravages of social blight. Responsibility started with the family and radiated out.

Out of this simple framework of values, they succeeded in forging a network of close-knit families tied to communities that emphasized self-help and cooperative ventures. There were protests against inequities, the most glaring of which was the brutally suppressed sugar strike of 1920. But there was really no time for revolutionary prescriptions even in ghettos where a secure environment and a thriving sense of personal and community identity provided important symbols of belongingness as hedges against outside hostility.

Perhaps there was nothing special about these people. Among other immigrants, they appeared quiet and quite ordinary. There were hoodlums, cheaters, and criminals among them. There was even a sprinkling of ultranationalists who believed that Japan could do no wrong. But somehow, the system obligated and compelled families and communities to take care of their own kind.

It was from just such an environment that Richard Sakakida and the others—members of the Japanese-American 100th Infantry Battalion, the 442d Regimental Combat Team, and the MIS—emerged to serve the United States during World War II.

To a man, they were sent off to war by parents who, in the spirit of their Japanese forebears, insisted that they die together or march home together after the war. Neither family nor community would tolerate anything less. For parents whose hopes for the future depended on their children, it was a matter of fate and duty, and their children understood.

Surprising as it may be, Sakakida received no medals or commendations for any of his heroic efforts as an undercover agent. He has accepted that as a consequence of being in undercover work and he has never complained. Perhaps he felt that was his fate.

The all-Japanese-American 100th Infantry Battalion and the 442d Regimental Combat Team, which later merged into one unit, fought in Europe and became the most decorated unit of its size in U.S. military history. The unit earned seven Presidential Unit Citations, thirty-six Army Commendations, and eighty-seven Division Commendations. Included among the 18,143 individual decorations awarded to these men were 9,486 Purple Hearts, 52 Distinguished Service Crosses, 4,000 Bronze Stars, 560 Silver Stars, and one Congressional Medal of Honor.

This story is therefore more than a story of one man. It is the history of a number of Americans who were raised in an obscure corner of America. It is a story of a small part of an American democracy in the making at a critical juncture of history.

For Lt. Col. Richard Sakakida, USAF, Retired, there will never be a full escape from the physical and emotional trauma that he suffered as a POW. In spite of that, he hopes that this story will somehow convey a message of forgiveness.

Finally, it should be noted that the word *issei* used throughout the book refers to the first generation of immigrants to arrive from Japan. The word *nisei* refers to the second generation of Japanese-Americans in America. The word *haole*, which is commonly used in Hawaii, refers to anyone who is Caucasian. It has come to mean that even though the generic meaning of the word in the Hawaiian language is "foreigner."

ACKNOWLEDGMENTS

I would like to acknowledge the extraordinary cooperation and assistance provided by Richard Sakakida while this book was being written. It must have been a difficult and painful task for him. The wholehearted support and understanding of his wife, Cherry, was indispensable.

I am particularly grateful to Lt. Gen. William J. McCaffrey, U.S. Army, Retired, and his wife, Mary, who took the time to read the manuscript; their advice and comments were invaluable. They were generous in providing the encouragement and moral support that were essential to the completion of this book.

I was also heartened by the generous support and encouragement provided throughout the writing of this book by U.S. Sen. Daniel K. Akaka of Hawaii and his legislative assistant, John A. Tagami.

I am also greatly indebted to my daughter, Miki, who provided the computer literacy that I lacked. She was always there when needed.

A special tribute is due to my wife, Jean, who was my best critic. Her tolerance through long periods of neglect and her endurance of my wayward temperament were vital from the beginning to the end of this project.

Finally, it should be noted that in spite of all the advice and suggestions I received from others, final responsibility for the composition of this book and for any mistakes contained therein, is mine alone.

Never in military history did an army know so much about the enemy prior to actual engagement.

Gen. Douglas MacArthur

The Nisei saved countless lives and shortened the war by two years.

Maj. Gen. Charles Willoughby

If you Japanese-Americans are ever questioned as to your loyalty, don't even bother to reply.

Maj. Gen. Clayton Bissell

Chapter 1

BRINGING UP THE PAST

It was a typical fall day in Fremont, California. The sun shone, casting its bright rays over our entire back yard. Leaves rustled in the breeze, flowers flourished in sunlit splendor, and our manicured lawn was a pleasure to behold. As Hildi, our pet dachshund, returned from her periodic inspection of our premises, a cool breeze wafted into the screened patio where we were seated.

On that fall day, we sat on our sun-drenched patio enjoying our ritual midafternoon break with snacks and cold drinks. The languid midafternoon lull of a warm fall day in California was something to be savored. It was a time when things slowed to a crawl.

Suddenly, the quiet spell was broken, as Hildi leaped onto the floor and began pacing restlessly as if in fear of some impending event. Little did we realize that we were soon to be visited by an echo from the past.

The telephone rang, and my wife, Cherry, quickly rose to get it.

Soon, I heard her say, "Dick, it's for you. A man named Tom Sakamoto wants to speak to you."

As I passed her on the way to the phone, I said, "Gee, I don't know anyone by that name."

21

My caller identified himself as a friend of a friend. He had heard about my contributions to American intelligence during World War II and he was calling me on behalf of an organization of Japanese-American veterans representing the Military Intelligence Service (MIS). He explained that the organization was made up of veterans who had served in the Pacific and China-Burma-India theaters of war during World War II.

He wasted no time in getting to the point. "Would you be willing to be the featured speaker at the fiftieth anniversary observance of the founding of the MIS?" he inquired.

Instinctively, I demurred. I don't like giving speeches, and as a former prisoner of war (POW), I was wary of being roped into anything involving unfamiliar people and organizations. I backed off at the outset by telling him that I had never served in the MIS, and I thought an MIS member would be better qualified to deliver the speech. But that didn't seem to deter him, so I did the next best thing: I told him that I would think about it and get back to him.

After hanging up, I wondered, "Do I need this?" Retirement had been good for me. After thirty-five years of military service, my wife and I had settled on Fremont as our place of retirement because of its proximity to San Francisco, military hospitals, commissaries, base exchanges, a veteran's hospital, and, yes, good sushi. Many of my former colleagues had doubted that I could leave work behind and settle down to a life of leisure. They were wrong. I had spent many exciting years first with the U.S. Army and then with the Office of Special Investigation of the U.S. Air Force, but that was a thing of the past. Besides, much of the trauma from my years as a prisoner of war had receded into a zone of tolerance in my memory bank during retirement, and I was very grateful for that. The call did trigger a sense of uncertainty but it had nothing to do with conventional fear. I had faced fear often enough to be sure of that. The uncertainty had to do with recalling a painful time that was buried in my subconscious, and I wanted to keep it there. There were things that even Cherry was unaware of.

Why? Because I had always kept my vow of secrecy and it was part of my heritage to keep personal feelings to myself and be a good soldier about it. Fifty years ago, that was the way things were done.

When I returned to the patio, Hildi had stopped pacing and was back in Cherry's lap.

I told Cherry about the invitation to speak at the MIS convention. "Oh, that's nice," she replied, which was her way of being noncommittal until she was sure about how I really felt. More than anyone else, she knew the implications of accepting such an invitation—there was more to it than just a simple yes or no.

I hadn't spoken publicly about my past because until 1972, information about my mission was classified. Even after that, getting the story out with all of its associated trauma and facing up to all of that seemed overwhelming. So, it was not just a matter of talking about the past. Could I and should I do it?

I let the decision of the MIS convention percolate in my mind for a few days. The issue bobbed to the surface intermittently at first. But in time, it took on an urgency of its own, welling up with increasing frequency. The speech began to appeal to me.

Cherry began to sense I was ready to reexamine the past. She encouraged me, "Why don't you give it a try?" The decision was finally made, and I called Tom Sakamoto to accept the invitation to speak.

To help me along, Cherry bought me a word processor. I am not much at divining metaphors, and, the computer itself presented a huge obstacle for a man who had spent his entire working life communicating with pencils and typewriters. But I had one thing going for me: military life had taught me to follow instructions. Before long, I had the hang of the word processor.

The technical problems were nothing compared to the mind games that followed. It was tough just organizing an outline as a myriad of thoughts raced through my mind vying for attention. It was like a dialectic without end.

So I retreated to my personal military file. I was a real GI when it came to keeping those things in order. One thought, one sentence at a time. "Keep it simple," I thought to myself, but it wasn't that easy. I was out of practice with writing and composing and, somehow, my mind kept wandering. I had to get back to a more disciplined frame of mind.

Soon I had a system. As I examined the file more carefully, each piece of the record began to evoke memories that had lain dormant over the years. Before long, emotions associated with each episode came back. I proceded carefully, and it wasn't so bad.

The first draft was a jumble of thoughts in search of some kind of order, and it was the size of a book. The first time around, I learned that coherent thoughts flashing through my mind had a way of disappearing when committed to the word processor. It's tough to write as fast as one thinks. The situation is worse on a small screen computer that scrolls sentences away as fast as they appear. But by the time I began condensing my book of thoughts and events into a concise speech, I was on a roll.

I had about a year to get ready. By the end of summer, I had a viable draft in hand but it was still too long. I spent the final month trimming and refining it. I also had to prime myself to deliver the speech to an unfamiliar audience. Meanwhile, the pressure mounted.

Composing the speech that I finally delivered was far more complex and difficult than I had ever imagined. But it was a liberating experience. It forced me to unburden myself of thoughts and emotions that had long festered inside of me. In coming to terms with the events and trauma, I had developed a new perspective.

However, the stress of what I was doing had begun to show. Cherry began to notice that I was waking up, trembling and perspiring in the middle of the night. Actually, it had happened all along, but it had not been as obvious before the call.

Growing up in Hawaii, I had learned about *gaman*, or the need to endure even the seemingly unendurable. I was proud of that trait, since it made me a better American in the process. It brought me closer to an understanding of who I am as a *nisei* American and what I stand for.

The joggers had it right when they used the phrase, "No pain, no gain." Over fifty years after the fact, pain and trauma were transformed into self-realization. And I was grateful for that.

Chapter 2

GROWING UP IN HAWAII

It all began 19 November 1920, in Puunene, Maui. I was born into the plantation life typical of the islands at that time. My father was employed in the boiler room of the sugar mill. Times were hard, but a newborn was a reaffirmation of life, hope, and continuance even in the hardest of times. In my family, my arrival mattered and that in itself was to make all the difference in the world.

I was the third son of Isoji and Kiku Sakakida, natives of Hiroshima, Japan, who immigrated to Hawaii in early 1900. When I was three, my family moved to Honolulu on the island of Oahu, where my father went to work for the Interisland Steamship Company. For my parents, the lure was economic betterment and a more comfortable life for all of us. Since I left Puunene as an infant, I had almost no recollection of what life was like there. But the connection to life on the plantation is important because the plantations provided the setting for the creation of the *issei* culture, which impacted on so many of us. So it was that I came to the city, and it was there that I was raised and educated.

I attended Kaiulani Elementary School, Kalakaua Junior High,

25

Central Intermediate School, and McKinley High School. At the same time, like many other *nisei* children, I attended Japanese language schools.

In those days, Honolulu was a vastly different place from what it is today. It was essentially a sleepy town even though it was regarded as the "big town" by people residing in the outlying islands. Downtown Honolulu was dominated by landmarks such as the Aloha Tower, Honolulu Harbor where luxury liners docked, Bishop Street with imposing office buildings, pleasing public parks, and imposing public buildings. For the tourists on the beaches of Waikiki, there was Diamond Head, a promontory towering above the ocean on the south side of the island. Restaurants, theaters, and small businesses abounded; and the Alexander Young Hotel, where managers of sugar, pineapple, and ranching operations on other islands stayed for their business meetings in Honolulu, and a more diverse blend of people on the streets gave the place a cosmopolitan feeling lacking in towns on the other islands.

The main artery through town was King Street over which buses and street cars traveled. And just as Bishop Street symbolized the mercantile interests in Hawaii, Fort Street was the mecca of shopping. Stores like Liberty House, McInernys, Watamull's, Kramers, and Sato Clothiers beckoned shoppers from all over the island. Along the waterfront, where fishing boats docked and fish markets thrived, the air was scented with the riches of the sea. There was also Chinatown, a colorful and vibrant area that was always teeming with people and entrepreneurial vigor. The aroma of Chinatown was a heady blend of exotic produce and imaginative cooking. The drab buildings masked a dynamic that set the Chinese communities apart from the Japanese. Early on, the Chinese established themselves as investors, and the Japanese were seen as conservative savers.

I grew up in a neighborhood of Honolulu called Palama, located inland from the coastal beach area and just a few miles from the central downtown area. It was a community of blue- and white-collar family homes with a scattering of mom-and-pop stores. The community boasted an outdoor movie theater that was enclosed on fall sides with sheets of corrugated iron. When it rained, everyone got wet. It was a time when status symbols meant little, at least as far as the kids were concerned. We felt that everyone was in the same boat. As a result, it was not just a place where we lived. Palama also provided a state of mind; a home turf that we could identify with. Whatever its faults, it was a good place to grow up.

Although residential mobility was far more fluid in Honolulu than in the outlying areas, youngsters tended to identify themselves in terms of their home districts and schools. Turf boundaries defined one's circle of friends or gang affiliations. The gangs in Palama were tough and street rules were strictly observed. One had to grow up tough in the neighborhood; it was taken for granted. The gym at Palama Settlement spawned some of the best amateur boxers in the islands. At an early age, I identified with and drew upon a community pride that was intense.

The homes in Palama were modest but comfortable and quite substantial for all family needs. Our home was always kept spick-and-span; the whole family seemed to thrive on that. Everyone contributed to family chores. Our house was more than just a home. It was a sanctuary where we learned social responsibility, family responsibility, and accountability.

The neighborhood was lush with greenery and tropical plants. But most of the children tended to take the hibiscus, bougainvillea, and plumeria for granted because they grew in such profusion all over the island. However, our interaction with nature was intimate. Mangoes, guavas, papayas, and other fruits grew on trees in our yards. In some places on the island, fruits grew wild and were there for the taking. Now and then we secretly helped ourselves to fruits off of our neighbors' tree. Sometimes, we got caught and were punished, but that, too, was part of growing up in Palama.

Palama was a predominantly Japanese community, but there were Chinese, Hawaiian, Filipino, Portuguese and Puerto Rican families living there too. Ethnic groups tended to stay among their own kind, especially when it involved intimate family matters. There was very little intermarriage. Economic survival and progress necessitated a pooling of resources and the family served as the single most important economic unit to do that.

People got along very well and even though most of the first-generation parents from the various ethnic groups did not speak much English, they managed to communicate with bits of English and words drawn from their own native languages. In the process, a pidgin language evolved, which was English mixed with all kinds of ethnic words and expressions. There was no formal grammatical structure to the language, and it was rich in nuances. Pidgin was the street language; it brought the kids from different ethnic groups closer together, and eventually, it became a badge of identity that all Hawaiian children shared. In school, the children used standard English but out of the classroom, pidgin was the medium of communication. English teachers used to regard pidgin English as a curse on the communication skills of the children of Hawaii. It didn't matter to us; we still persisted in "talking pidgin."

As a child, I walked to school every day with the other children in the neighborhood. There were few cars and it was safe. We walked several miles but nobody seemed to mind. There was no school busing as we know it today. All of the children carried lunches to school. However, among the boys, the lunches never lasted until lunchtime. By midmorning recess, most of the lunches were eaten, which allowed us to spend more time playing during the regular lunch hour. For most of the kids, there was not much time to play after school, so lunch hours were precious. The girls suffered because we asked them to give us part of their lunches so we wouldn't go hungry all afternoon.

My parents were typical of their generation. They thought of themselves as Japanese. Most of the first-generation Japanese, the *isseis*, had intended to return to Japan when they first arrived in the islands. They planned to earn and save as much of their wages as possible and then return to Japan to buy land and homes there. For that reason, many of them did not invest in property in Hawaii.

Many of the first-generation immigrants came to Hawaii without much formal education. They all spoke Japanese but many could not read or write in Japanese. They got news about Japan from the local Japanese-language radio programs, or heard about events from friends who were able to read and write. Because of this, most Japanese immigrants insisted on the education of their children. *Isseis* revered their heritage and believed that a child was not properly educated without schooling in the Japanese language. Parents who could afford it sent their children to Japan for advanced schooling. Sometimes, they were sent right after their primary school education in Hawaii.

I went to Japanese-language school as a matter of course, starting in first grade. My parents decreed that I go and I went. They never stopped to consider what I would do with Japanese-language skills in an English-speaking country.

The Hongwanji Japanese School that I attended was considered the best in Hawaii. The tuition was $4.50 per month—a lot of money considering that field laborers earned a meager $18.00 per month. My father's salary exceeded what the field laborers earned, but still, the tuition was high.

The school was staffed by Buddhist priests of the Shinshu sect who had been trained in Japan and were generally graduates of the Otani Buddhist University in Kyoto. There was no evangelical fervor to their teachings. Instead, their intensity was reflected in the very quiet way they seemed to control every observable facet of their behavior. Their emotions and bodily movements were always held in check. They eschewed violence for the sake of violence, but we always sensed that there was a response of fierce intensity waiting to be unleashed if they were provoked. They taught us a great deal about emotional and physical control and endurance.

Classes were held Monday through Friday after the classes at our English-language public schools. They lasted from one to two hours a day. On Saturdays, classes were held from 8:00 A.M. to noon.

Japanese schools were not popular among the children. It was much easier to speak English, and besides, Japanese classes cut in on play time. Most of the young people, if they had their way, preferred to spend their time with sports, jobs, or just hanging out with their peers. But for the communities at large, there were distinct social benefits. The long school day provided a disciplined environment for growth and it kept some of the more unruly elements off of the streets.

29

Throughout my school years, I did all of the homework assigned by my public school and Japanese school teachers. Semester exams at both schools often coincided, adding to the strain of keeping up with studies. The teachers at the Japanese schools were strict, and students were disciplined with physical punishment. Disobedient students were slapped at will. Parents supported the teachers, not their children, and when they heard of misbehavior at school, they punished their children at home, as well.

At many of the schools, teachers who were experts in *kendo,* the art of swordsmanship, would bludgeon troublemaking students into submission with bamboo swords. It was akin to an old boxing champion taking a brash youngster into a boxing ring to teach him a lesson. It was all very legal. It was also an effective discipline.

The Japanese school curriculum adhered closely to models established in Japan. The students were taught about the divine origins of the Japanese islands and about the ancestral ties between the Sun Goddess and the Imperial Family. Years later, I asked a former teacher who was a priest whether he believed what he had taught the children. He admitted that he did not believe the story, but he emphasized that the curriculum demanded it, and he did what he was required to do. Besides, mythology played an important part in the instruction of children.

In addition to reading and writing, the Hongwanji School offered courses in composition, advanced reading skills, and literary Japanese, as well as training in the use of the abacus. History and ethics were important parts of the curriculum. There were no libraries at the Japanese schools so students were forced to rely primarily on textbooks. Lectures were given on morality and ethics with an emphasis on virtue, filial piety, honor, and integrity. Classical tales and popular stories were used to provide role models for students to emulate. The materials, developed in Japan to raise generations of loyal citizens, were used in Hawaii even though there was no allegiance to the Japanese emperor. In Hawaii, the Japanese schools may have created a generation of students who used their lessons in becoming better Americans. There was heavy emphasis on classical subjects and no discussion of current events in Japan.

Perhaps because the school was run by a Buddhist order, the classes on ethics did not stress military values as was the case in Japan during that period. *Bushido,* the code of the warrior, was ignored in our class on ethics. That was because Buddhism in general stressed compassion and opposition to warlike activities. It was also probably due to the traditional tensions that existed between Buddhism and militarism. During the sixteenth century, Oda Nobunaga, the reigning military ruler in Japan, slaughtered thousands of Buddhist priests and burned down all of the major temples around the capital city of Kyoto when the priests stubbornly refused to worship him instead of Buddha. However, as children, we were often regaled by our parents with stories about the great samurais, which made us admire them as much as we did American cowboys. The impact of Buddhism was undeniable in spite of the historical conflicts between state and temple. Zen Buddhism in particular taught the samurais to become self-reliant, ascetic in training, and totally focused as fighters for dedicated causes. For the *niseis,* anyway, the multicultural education that we valued was provided at home, not in the classroom.

The first-generation Japanese were aware of what Japanese aggression could mean to their own fortunes in America. Moreover, life in Hawaii, in close proximity to other racial and ethnic groups, made them far more internationalist in their outlook than the more insular and in some cases xenophobic brethren in Japan during the politically turbulent 1930s.

By the time I graduated from Japanese school, I regarded my reading knowledge of Japanese to be fair. However, later on, when the U.S. Army tested me on some Japanese documents, I was able to handle them without much difficulty.

My speaking knowledge, by Japanese standards, left a lot to be desired, however. That was because my first exposure to spoken Japanese was the Hiroshima dialect that my family and family friends spoke rather than the standard Japanese that the teachers taught. It was a problem that was common to my generation in Hawaii; what we learned to speak was *hogen,* a regional dialect. Furthermore, we did not know the proper terms of address for dif-

31

ferent classes of people. Terms used to address people of different rank, social status, age, and so on, all required special usages. This was something that educated Japanese natives learned early in life and were quite sensitive about. For them, it was a natural part of growing up, but the children of Hawaii were not exposed to it.

After the war, when I was involved with young second-generation *niseis* in the investigation of war crimes, I realized that their classroom Japanese was insufficient for them to be effective in their work. We faced a multitude of embarassments because they didn't know the finer points of usage—the class, gender, and status distinctions important to fluency. Clearly, our Japanese parents had taught us their language, but we had adopted another culture.

My Japanese school experience was lasting, but by far the greatest educational impact I felt was from the public school system of Hawaii. I attended classes with Asians, Hawaiians, and Caucasians, although most of the more affluent Caucasians went to private schools such as Punahou. The number of Caucasian students at McKinley High School was comparatively small but most of the faculty members were Caucasian.

During my high school years, world events reported in the English- and Japanese-language newspapers began to focus on Japan. That country's takeover of Manchuria in 1931 and its invasion of China in 1937 led to much speculation in Japanese news reports about the possibility of war between the United States and Japan. Yet, most of the people in the Japanese community did not regard the threats as matters of personal concern. People were too preoccupied with earning a living to be concerned with political and world events that seemed so remote. Some may have sensed that a confrontation would occur eventually but certainly not right away.

A discernible wave of anti-Japanese sentiment arose in the Chinese community in Honolulu during the Manchurian incident. The response to the Japanese aggression was palpably negative in spite of the island environment where people tended to keep their thoughts to themselves. In some cases, the reaction was notable for its virulence, resulting in one particularly memorable rumor that the proprietors of Chinese restaurants were grinding glass to put into food served to Japanese customers in retaliation for the events in Manchuria. For a while, therefore, the Japanese patronage of Chinese restaurants, which was traditionally heavy, declined precipitously. Many of the restaurants nearly went out of business as a result. It was an unfortunate situation for the children as well as the adults. They did not understand the conflict and they wondered why they were being drawn into something that was occurring halfway around the world. At the most elemental level, however, kids were kids, and friends were friends, and the *niseis* didn't feel any compunction about resenting what Japanese militarism was causing them to experience in Hawaii.

As I neared the end of my senior year at McKinley High, I needed to decide what to do after graduation. I was presented with various career alternatives. In Japanese school, I was appointed president of my class because of my class record. The principal of the school, who was also a priest, wanted me to be the first Japanese-American to formally enter a Buddhist religious order. He spoke to my mother, who had been widowed many years before, about the matter, offering me a scholarship towards a university education at the Buddhist order's college in Kyoto with an eye toward eventual ordination by the church. My father's death when I was age seven had left my mother alone to decide on my future, and she was receptive to the idea. However, at the same time, another option appeared through the ROTC program at McKinley High School.

During that time, ROTC was a two-year requirement at McKinley. Sophomores who passed their physical examinations had two options: ROTC or the school band. The choice was clear—my mother could not afford to buy me a musical instrument so I opted for ROTC.

ROTC classes lasted an hour and were held three days a week. During the first year of training, the instructions centered on handling rifles and performing close order drills. The second year was spent on such things as map reading and military tactics.

The professor of military science and tactics at McKinley High was Col. Walter Gilbert, a veteran of World War I. After the armistice of 1918, he reverted to his permanent rank of major before resuming his career in the peacetime army. Once he was posted at McKinley High, he became a primary force in the development of its ROTC program. One of Colonel Gilbert's responsibilities was to select a cadet officer corps from among the ROTC cadets. He had apparently observed my performance and, to my surprise, he asked me to return for my senior year with the ROTC as a cadet officer. I quickly accepted his offer. The decision to appoint a cadet colonel rested in the hands of a faculty board. Colonel Gilbert was persuasive in arguing that I was the best qualified cadet, and the board went along. I was appointed cadet colonel for the 1938–39 academic year. As the cadet colonel, I led the brigade, which included three regiments of roughly 1,500 cadets. I directed the formation of troops for parades and was also entrusted with disciplinary responsibilities for the brigade.

In his capacity as the senior ROTC instructor for the Hawaiian Islands, the colonel also had the privilege of nominating an outstanding cadet for entry into West Point. He offered me the opportunity to become the first *nisei* to enter the U.S. Military Academy. So, in addition to the Buddhist option, I had a military option to consider.

Ultimately, I took neither of the options. My mother was against West Point. At that time, the Japanese community did not hold the military in high regard. It had the mistaken notion that the military was only for those who couldn't make it in civilian life. Somehow, they could not envision me among officers and gentlemen; only among the porters and spear carriers that they saw in the old samurai movies. Besides, a working son represented a hedge against financial difficulty among immigrant families. Whatever the reason, I was an obedient son and my chance at West Point regrettably went by the wayside.

At the same time, I had no real desire to become a Buddhist priest either. The church offered to finance my education but I shuddered at the thought of being regarded as a square and being tied down irrevocably to a long-term commitment. Educational programs at the church depended largely on private contributions and I was loathe to be forever obligated to such donors.

My other choice was to join the local police force. The colonel was again helpful and arranged an interview for me with his friend, a captain in the Honolulu Police Department. The interview was cordial, but the captain advised me to gain some weight and to come back at age twenty-one.

The summer after graduating from high school, I worked at the Hawaiian Pineapple Company. Most students worked at the pineapple canneries around Honolulu during the summer months. The pay was good and the job allowed us to work full-time for three months during the summer.

One day during the summer, radio station KGU advertised an opening for a Japanese-language announcer. At the insistence of my sister, I went to the station for an interview. I took a test, was hired on the spot, and began work the next morning. My job was to do the commercials. The program was on the air daily for one hour only, so I held onto my day job at the cannery, working 6:00 P.M. to 6:00 A.M. Once I got the job at KGU however, I was allowed to leave my cannery shift early enough to get to the radio station on time. My routine was to get off work at the cannery, walk the four miles to KGU, and get there just in time to do the broadcast. After my summer stint at the cannery ended, I continued announcing at KGU and began looking for another job.

A referral from a family friend eventually led to a job at Asahi Furniture Company, working in warehouse delivery. My job was to go to the wharf, load the incoming shipments onto the truck, and then haul them back to the company warehouse. For that, I was paid eighty dollars a month.

My daily allowance for lunch was twenty-five cents, which was enough to pay for lunch at a restaurant in those days. Some of us bought lunch from the food vendors who sold meals out of carts that they pushed around town. One favorite dish was beef stew over rice, which cost a dime. There was not much beef in the greasy stew, but it was tasty and filling.

A nickle went a long way too. After a hard day of hauling furniture, my partner and I used to stop off at a bakery where a former classmate worked. For a nickle, we could buy a bag full of day-old pastries and a large coke to wash them down.

After a year at Asahi Furniture, I heard of an opening at American Factors, a huge wholesale conglomerate, through another friend of the family. I was hired as a stock clerk at twice the salary that I earned at Asahi Furniture. I was elated at the prospect of being paid eighty dollars twice a month! American Factors was a large, rock-solid company and promotion prospects were good, so I was content to be there. It allowed me to help my family financially and have the time to indulge in a bit of carefree recreation for a change. I assumed that I would be settling into a very easy and comfortable lifestyle.

In 1939, few if any of the residents of our community were aware of the events that were leading up to war between the United States and Japan. I myself was far too preoccupied with the novelty of my new life to think about events brewing in Europe and Asia. After years of school, which had left me with little time for play or leisure, I felt justified in focusing on personal enjoyment. I had money in my pocket, free evenings, new clothes, and time for girls and dates.

By the summer of 1939, war had already engulfed Europe. It began with Hitler's invasion of Poland on 1 September 1939, which compelled England and France to declare war on Germany. America remained neutral at the outset in accordance with the special legislation on neutrality adopted by Congress in 1937. But by openly abrogating some basic tenets of international law and the neutrality rights of other nations, Hitler in effect signaled an intent to declare war against all existing democracies. It provided just the impetus needed in the United States to arouse public concern about the looming threat. Gradually, the traditional reliance on a policy of neutrality began to wane in the United States.

In the streets of Honolulu, life went on as usual. The languor that hung over the city was as commonplace as the trade winds that constantly graced the island of Oahu. Waikiki and its exclusive hotels were the playground of the very rich and famous and were therefore off-limits to the locals. The only sign of a military presence was seen on weekends. The army and navy officers headed for Waikiki and the enlisted men congregated around the strip joints and watering holes in the downtown area.

On Mondays, everything returned to normal. The soldiers went back to their bases and the people of Honolulu returned to work. I felt very much a part of that workforce. To me, there was very little indication that life could ever be any different from what it was then.

Chapter 3

RECRUITMENT IN SECRECY

B y February 1941, I had settled into what looked like a promising career track. Life had taken on a comfortable pattern: up at the crack of dawn, a hurried breakfast prepared by my mother, and a long brisk walk to work. It was a daily ritual, but life as I knew it then was anything but humdrum.

I enjoyed the novelty of work, and above all, I liked being paid to work. It was satisfying to be able to contribute to the support of the family. Children in the Japanese communities customarily turned over all of their earnings to their parents. I was no different. It was a point of pride for me to regularly turn my earnings over to my mother, particularly since my father had died when I was a child. My mother would then give me an allowance to take care of my food and recreation needs.

My place of employment was several miles from my home. I was a brisk walker, intent on getting to work on time. Actually, I always managed to get there ahead of time, something that became a life-long habit. Years later, I saw the same tendency in Tokyo, where everyone rushed to get to work. I noticed that nobody strolled along. Everyone seemed to be at half trot or more. I probably looked just like that to others on the streets of Honolulu.

By the time I got to downtown Honolulu, the city was alive with activity. It was easy to get caught up in the excitement of the city as I joined in the flow of people who crowded the streets at the beginning of the day. However, there was also the seamier side of life to behold as I hurried along. There were people for whom life was not so easy, and there were many people caught in futureless situations. In the islands, even among the young men of my age, dead-end jobs, family obligations, and social pressures had a way of eroding individual dreams and ambitions. All around me it was happening, but I did not imagine it happening to me. I had steady eight-to-five job with prospects for advancement, and I was determined to build on that for the future.

The American Factors Warehouse where I worked was located on Honolulu Harbor, right across from the Aloha Tower. One day, late in February 1941, it was, as usual, still very quiet when I got to the warehouse premises. It was a beautiful time of day, with a bracingly cool breeze blowing over the docks bringing with it the refreshing smell of the ocean. The familiar sounds of waves lapping against the hulls of ships anchored in their berths and of ropes creaking and stretching with every gust of ocean wind drew attention to the quiet waterfront so early in the morning. But the quiet never lasted. The moment the men with their machinery arrived to work the docks, it was sheer bedlam. It always began with the morning work whistle. Like everyone else, I immediately set about the tasks of the day.

The moment the workday began, the warehouse was a beehive of activity and a cacophony of sounds. Trucks and forklifts moved in and out of the building, people shouted to be heard above the din, and there was the never-ending jangle of telephones ringing. Calls directed to me usually involved requisitions, work orders, hand receipts, bills of lading, and nomenclature searches. The operational procedures governing my work were orderly but the flow of requests were never so. For some reason, every request was a hurried request. Everything was needed by yeserday.

However, one telephone call I received early in the afternoon on that fateful day in February transformed my entire life. I had just finished eating one of those hot lunches off of a push cart when the phone rang.

I was startled to hear the voice of my old ROTC instructor. "This is Colonel Gilbert," he said. "I want you to report to Central Intermediate School tomorrow morning. I won't be there but everything has been arranged." Although I had no remaining ties with ROTC, I felt I was receiving an order that I could not refuse. When I said I had to check with my department head, he told me he had already spoken to him and that approval had already been given.

I wanted to ask him why, but the whole drift and tone of the brief conversation indicated that he preferred not to elaborate on the matter over the phone.

His final question was, "Do you still want to leave the islands to travel elsewhere?" To which I replied in the affirmative since I had often confided in private to him about wanting to go to the mainland someday. "I think I have just the thing for you, so be there," he said before hanging up.

I immediately went to my department head to make sure that I had his permission to make the appointment on the next day. "You have my permission to go," he said. I began thinking that something important must be in the offing.

I walked home as usual after work that afternoon, thoroughly absorbed in thought. By the time I got home, a thousand possibilities, all good, had occurred to me. In my mind, there was no room for pessimism. I decided not to tell anyone in my family about the impending meeting and throughout supper, I wondered what was in store for me. That night, I decided to stay home and turn in early instead of going out with friends. I went to bed charged with anticipation of what the mysterious meeting might be about.

Next morning I went through my usual workday routine. However, after breakfast, I walked to Central Intermediate School instead of American Factors. When I arrived, I was immediately taken to my appointment. Everything seemed prearranged to precision.

I was whisked into a room in the administrative wing of the school building where a group of men sat, awaiting my arrival. I was surprised to see uniformed army and navy officers who, with nary an introduction or explanation, started questioning me.

I realized then that I was being put through a formal interview. But for what, I still had no idea.

41

The interview board consisted of about six very self-assured military officers—they were primarily from the navy but the army was there too, as far as I could tell.

When I first entered the office, I was daunted by the prospect of facing such an imposing looking panel. The officers said very little about themselves other than that they had come to Hawaii for the interviews from Washington, D.C. Never having been off of the islands, I was impressed.

I was also in for a big surprise. To my astonishment, the entire interview was conducted in Japanese. It was mind-boggling to hear Japanese being spoken so fluently by *haoles*. Each of them had apparently been to Japan to study the language and learn about the country. They exhibited a civility that was common to Japanese culture—even their gestures were correct. The questions were tough and to the point, but all along, they went out of their way to make me feel comfortable.

I was questioned for an entire day. They wanted to know everything about me and my parents. They also gave me a Japanese-language examination that lasted three full days. In addition to extended oral exams, I was given a series of written tests including standard translations from Japanese to English and reverse translations from English to Japanese. It was a grueling process that left me exhausted at the end of each day.

There were approximately thirty candidates being tested and interviewed at the same time. I was the youngest and the only one who was not a graduate of the University of Hawaii.

At the conclusion of our testing, they sent us home and promised test results in about two weeks. Even then, none of us had been informed of the purpose of all this testing or of the secrecy. All of us were tested separately, so there was no time at the end of the day to compare notes or get acquainted with each other.

I, for one, was sufficiently intimidated by the whole experience to remain silent. At that age, I was still closely tied to the feudal notion of not questioning authority. My own carefully guarded hunch, based purely on wishful thinking, was that the job would take the successful candidates to a major metropolis on the mainland. For me, Los Angeles would have been the assignment of choice. But for the meantime, I went back to my job.

Two weeks later, Colonel Gilbert called again at work.

"Richard, I've got good news for you. You made it," he said without hesitation. I was barely able to contain myself as I felt a surge of excitement pass through me.

"Thank you sir, that is good news," I blurted out. The colonel chuckled and went on to say, "Congratulations—you did well and I'm glad I sponsored you."

He continued on, adding, "You are the primary pick. There were only two men selected. The other was Arthur Komori. An appointment has been set up for you on March 13." He also said he would pick me up and drive me to the appointment.

After I hung up, I realized that I had again forgotten to ask the colonel what all of this was about. I cursed that mental lapse but I was still buoyed by a dream of going to the States. Besides, I trusted Colonel Gilbert to look after my best interests. In all of my dealings with him, I had never had any reason to doubt him. There was some uncertainty in my mind, since I didn't know for sure what they wanted, but the thought of going abroad, changing my lifestyle, and possibly finding adventure excited me. I gave no thought to turning back.

That night, I informed my mother that Colonel Gilbert was coming over to pick me up in the morning for some sort of job interview. I told her there was a possibility that I would be leaving home. She was not happy about the uncertainty, but she felt helpless to object too strongly. Predictably, she lapsed into silence, choosing the way of a recluse to await the results of my interview.

On the morning of 13 March 1941, the colonel arrived bright and early to drive me to the interview. "Good morning Richard," he gushed as I got into his car. He was in high spirits and did most of the talking. I waited for him to explain everything to me but he said nothing about the impending meeting, nor did he tell me where we were headed.

So finally we rode in silence through the Honolulu traffic. "Look," he said suddenly, "the sun's coming out. I hope that's a good omen." I agreed. The winter rain had cast a pall over Palama and it was nice to see the sun peeking out again through the clouds. Rain was good for plants and flowers but too much rain was depressing. Too much rain was also especially bad for the mangoes and papayas. As we drove on, it occurred to me that just as the plants had no control over Mother Nature, I had no control over my own fate at the moment. It was not a cheerful thought and it only added to my reticence.

By the time we reached King Street, the sun was out in full force. Colonel Gilbert seemed aware of the quiet unease that had settled over me and he tried to draw me out but it was to no avail. I could not say what was on my mind, so we drove in silence. Perhaps I was afraid, perhaps I trusted him, perhaps he seemed like a parent to me. Regardless, I had been taught to obey without question, so that's what I did.

Before long, we were on Dillingham Boulevard, heading out of the downtown area. Soon, we turned into the front entrance of Fort Shafter where a military policeman stood guard. When he spotted Colonel Gilbert's windshield sticker, which identified him as an officer, he saluted smartly and waved us through.

Fort Shafter is situated a few miles from downtown Honolulu on acres of greenery, flowering shrubs, and trees. The monkeypod trees near the gate provided pleasant shade from the sun, which was by then warming everything in sight. It was as if the Hawaiian gods had suddenly parted the curtain of dark clouds to let the sun in. Fuschia, gold, and yellow hibiscus and bougainvillea bushes, neatly trimmed to match the well-tended emerald lawns, surrounded the buildings along the driveway. The smell of fresh trade winds mixed with the perfume of flowers. Even natives are sometimes mesmerized by the natural beauty of the islands.

Colonel Gilbert parked in front of a building with a sign that read, "Headquarters, Hawaiian Department, United States Army." He got out, beckoned me to follow him, and walked into an office marked "G2." This was my introduction to army intelligence, the information-gathering branch of the service.

We entered the office of Colonel Marston, the head of G2. The noncommissioned officer (noncom) in charge said the colonel was expecting us. "Sounds urgent," I thought to myself.

Colonel Marston graciously invited us into his office. He appeared to be a real gentleman, low-key and very self-assured. I expected the visit to be purely ceremonial. Colonel Marston congratulated me on my selection and told me that the tests and interviews were rigorous by design and that it was a credit to me that I had made it to the top of the selection list. In my mind, I kept wondering, selection for what? But I said nothing.

He then got to what he referred to as the final order of business, which was to swear me in. Swearing in for what? I thought to myself, but things were moving along so fast that I didn't dare ask. I was dealing with two colonels, and I respected rank and elders. I didn't realize that I was being sworn in as a special agent. This was a task customarily performed by the G2 himself, but on this occasion, he departed from custom and asked Colonel Gilbert to perform the honors instead. Undoubtedly, the colonel wanted to recognize the role that Gilbert played in recruiting me for G2. Colonel Marston stood and watched as I was sworn in. For the first time, I realized for sure that it was the U.S. Army that wanted me.

As we left Fort Shafter, Colonel Gilbert seemed uncharacteristically ebullient.

"Good work, Richard, I knew you could make it," he said. "I had all the faith in the world in you."

"Thank you sir," I replied. "I actually owe it all to you."

"Nonsense," he shot back, "you earned it." Actually, I was yearning for an explanation of why he hadn't told me I was to be sworn into the U.S. Army. As we headed back to town in his car, I began to collect my thoughts and I was struck by something that had completely escaped me during the excitement. I turned to him and said, "Sir, I think I got a problem."

"What is it?" he asked.

"I'm only twenty years old and I think I need my mother's consent to be in the army," I replied. Indeed, back then, anyone under twenty-one needed parental consent to join the army.

"Oh my God," muttered the colonel. "It never dawned on us. And here we thought we had every base covered."

After a brief moment of thought, he inquired, "Do you suppose I could stop by and see your mother today?" It was my turn to be caught off guard since I knew that mother was not expecting him to stop by. This must involve something big, I thought, since Colonel Gilbert was obviously bent on locking in my recruitment immediately.

"Sure you can stop by," I replied on impulse as we headed back to Palama. Actually, I really wasn't sure whether it was a good idea to catch my mother by surprise. Mother knew about the interview, but beyond that, she had no idea what to expect. When she heard the colonel's car stopping in front of our home, she peered through the window to see who it was.

The sight of me leading an army colonel into our home probably alarmed her—she spoke hardly any English, and she was not used to having *haole* visitors.

I brought in my guest and I said to my mother in Japanese, "Mother, this is Colonel Gilbert," at which point the colonel bowed. Reflexively, my mother got down on the floor on her hands and knees and bowed, head down. She was clearly flustered. The colonel also seemed somewhat at a loss as to what to do. She was being very Japanese, and all he could do was to smile amiably. To end that awkward encounter, I pointed Colonel Gilbert toward the living room.

In his Western way, Colonel Gilbert wasted no time getting to the point. My mother would have wanted to serve tea and sweets to set the tone for the unexpected visit. But he quickly proceeded to his request that she allow me, her youngest son, to join the U.S. Army.

My mother was aghast at the colonel's behavior and appalled by the thought of my joining the army.

However, the older generation perceived power in Hawaii to be vested in a WASP oligarchy, and though she knew little about Gilbert, the fact that he was Caucasian and a high-ranking officer made him seem more powerful than he was in reality. She too had been taught to submit to authority figures.

The colonel was persistent in his prodding. My mother's response was typical of her generation of Japanese women in Hawaii. She hid her true feelings behind a mask of stoic resignation. She occasionally glanced up at me, and I sensed that her feelings could be summarized in one short Japanese phrase: *shikata ga nai,* or "it can't be helped." I could see sadness in her face. The colonel wanted me in the army, and yet there was no war. "What's going on?" she must have wondered, as he kept reassuring her that everything would be fine and there was nothing to worry about. Hearing his promises, she finally relented and gave her consent.

As I watched her, I was touched by her plight. She knew I was committed to serve, so she had to let go. But it was not easy. It was just as hard for me as it was for her because I understood her dilemma and I could not help her.

My mother could not sign her name in English so the colonel advised her to mark an "X" where her signature was supposed to be. He then signed his name next to it to verify the consent. I did not realize the regret the colonel himself was experiencing. There was a matter of grave national security involved, which neither mother nor I was aware of, and he had no choice but to do his duty. My mother's consent was a fait accompli. I had been roped into the army even before her consent was granted, and I had a feeling that even if mother had refused, they would have found some way to keep me.

The papers formalizing my induction specified that I would be given an immediate rank of buck sergeant in the CIP.

I asked Colonel Gilbert what CIP stood for. "You mean you don't know?" he asked.

"No sir," I replied.

"It stands for Civilian Interpreter Police," he stated. Actually, he didn't know himself; it really stood for Corps of Intelligence Police.

"What do they do?" I continued.

The colonel's response was, "You shouldn't have any problem. Besides, you said you wanted to travel so give it a go. Your primary responsibility, as I understand it, is to listen to Japanese-language radio broadcasts, read the local Japanese-language newspapers, and report any information of interest to the U.S. Army. You'll be given a set of requirements when you get on the job."

I still assumed that I was slated for stateside duty, perhaps somewhere in the Los Angeles area. Soon thereafter, I was ordered to report back to the G2 office at Fort Shafter. When I got there, the G2 told me that my duty station would be the Philippines. I was stunned. "Why wasn't I told?" I asked myself. Of course, such a question was meaningless now. There was no way out. I felt I had trusted others and had been misled.

My orders stated that I would be departing for the Philippines on 7 April 1941, approximately three weeks after my somewhat surreptitious induction.

So, there I was, preparing to depart on a foreign assignment with no basic training and no instructions on what I was to do when I got there. Presumably, instructions would be forthcoming, but it was becoming increasingly difficult for me to operate on faith alone.

My orders said that I was not to talk to anyone about my destination except for members of my immediate family. My basic cover story, if I ever needed one among friends was a tenuous one—that I was leaving the islands to further my education. Moreover, there was to be no correspondence with anyone except my immediate family. Things were beginning to sound very ominous.

I quit my civilian job immediately after I was sworn into the army. Until the day prior to my departure, I reported to work at the Army Contact Office, located in the Federal Building in downtown Honolulu. The contact office provided a convenient cover for army operations. My training consisted of working with the radio and press media to ferret out information of counterintelligence value to the U.S. military. At that time, there was still a great deal of travel between Japan and Hawaii. The Hawaiian Command was interested in knowing who was traveling between Tokyo and Honolulu. But it was still peacetime and I was not fully aware of the implications of what I was doing.

Both I and Arthur Komori, who was also being sent to Manila, were informed that no one would be allowed to see us off at the docks. Even family members were forbidden to be there.

Since I was the youngest child in the family, my mother was heartbroken that I was leaving. She was more disturbed when she heard I was headed for the Philippines. She had a very distorted image of the Philippines and the Filipino people. One prevailing impression in Hawaii was that the Filipinos were highly temperamental and volatile people and were likely to draw knives whenever they felt threatened or put upon. Like most people, she had no idea that Manila, my destination, was called "The Pearl of the Orient" and that the wealth and glitter of Honolulu paled in comparison to Manila. Instead, she conjured up images of backward agriculture, water buffaloes, grass huts propped up on stilts, and little villages where violence was common.

On the day of my departure, Colonel Gilbert drove me to Honolulu Harbor. When he arrived to pick me up, my mother escorted me as far as the front gate of our home. She then said something to me that I will never forget. She told me, "In the event that my motherland goes to war with America, just remember that America is your country. Your father and your uncles all served in the Japanese Army with honor and I do not want you to return from service in the U.S. Army in disgrace." The unspoken part of that advice was that in order to uphold the family honor, one must be prepared to die willingly for one's country.

With those words, she patted me on the shoulder and sent me off. For the first-generation Japanese, any public display of affection was frowned on. There were no hugs or kisses. And like many of the strong and loving women of that generation, the most profuse and emotional shedding of tears would occur in the privacy of their homes. For the next three-and-a-half years, there would be countless sleepless nights for my mother as she worried about my whereabouts and safety.

I left sad and apprehensive about what lay ahead but, like her, I was determined not to let my emotions betray me. I would uphold the honor of the family name in the service of the United States of America. The powerful ties that bound parents to children in those days represented more than a mere hint of masochism. In the tight-knit Japanese communities of Hawaii, the *niseis* were sent off to war with heavy obligations to family, community, and nation. There was to be no shirking of responsibilities on the battlefield. It was painful for the *issei* parents to say it to their children, but it was nevertheless a matter of duty to tell them they must be prepared to give their lives in battle. To fail to do so would have brought shame into the home—a fate worse than death. This extraordinary commitment had to start with the parents themselves. Life was unfair for many of them, but that had nothing to do with upholding honor.

Chapter 4

ASSIGNMENT TO MANILA

In January 1941, preliminary negotiations had begun in Washington, D.C., between U.S. and Japanese envoys to try to defuse the rapidly growing tensions between the two countries. My recruitment began soon after that time, and by March, I was a member of the U.S. Army. Japan's continuing military incursions into China and Indochina in quest of a Greater East Asia Co-Prosperity Sphere never abated during the talks. A better assessment of Japan's true military intentions was therefore needed even as the talks got underway in Washington.

Hindsight tells us that war was imminent by then. But like most Hawaiians and millions of other Americans, I was blissfully ignorant of the impending crisis even as I was headed into it myself. Considering the circumstances, perhaps it was for the best.

Fortunately, the threat of war in Asia and the Pacific region was not lost on some of our leaders in the War Department in Washington. The urgency with which they recruited me offered proof of that. By the time of my departure for the Philippines, I knew that something big was up and one way or another, I would be involved in it. But the uncertainty about how and when that would occur was disconcerting and downright scary.

51

On 7 April 1941, the day that I left for the Philippines, I was driven to the pier by Colonel Gilbert. Since he was personally involved in my recruitment, he was intent on seeing me off. Throughout the drive to the pier, he offered words of reassurance.

It was obvious that he was concerned about rumors of the impending war and about what would happen to me if it came to pass. Since I no longer had a father, it was nice to have him along to give me some words of counsel. Hoping against hope but probably fearing the worst, he seemed to be in a melancholy mood as we drove through downtown Honolulu.

The colonel was a combat veteran of World War I, a brutal conflict that, in terms of the magnitude of death, destruction, and mayhem inflicted on the people of Europe, made people look upon it as a war to end all wars. What he experienced during the war was probably running through his head, for he was showing an uncharacteristic sadness and solicitousness in place of the tough and gruff image that he usually projected. To me, it was somewhat disconcerting to see this side of him.

Up to then, there had been no real personal bond between us. From the day of our very first encounter at McKinley High School, our relationship had always been very formal. He commanded; I obeyed as a soldier should. Neither of us would have it any other way. However, on that day, without a word or gesture, he made it clear to me that he cared a great deal about what war would do to me. I was grateful for that.

As we drove along King Street, I looked intently at the bustling street, shops, restaurants, and theaters, wondering when I would be able to walk the streets of Honolulu again. As we passed through the entrance to the harbor, I got another glimpse of the American Factors Warehouse where I worked. I felt like getting out to say goodbye to my friends and coworkers but that was not to be. Besides, they would never understand.

As we approached the pier, the colonel shook my hand and said, "Good luck to you. Take care of yourself. I'll just drop you off close to the pier so you can make your way to the ship without being seen by too many people." He gripped my hand firmly for a brief moment and then let go.

I quickly got out of the car and hurriedly made my way to the ship without looking back. When I got on board, someone directed me to my quarters, a cabin on the main deck that I was to share with Arthur Komori.

Since it was departure time, Komori and I went out to the deck to watch the proceedings. As I leaned on the railing, I noticed that Colonel Marston, the head of G2, was also at the pier to see us off. There was no hand waving, merely eye contact on the part of both sides to avoid any compromise of security.

Our ship was called the *Republic*. It was a German ship commandeered by the United States in the aftermath of World War I and pressed into service to transport U.S. troops around the Pacific. In its time, it was a highly regarded vessel capable of doing twenty knots, which was quite fast for a ship of its class. The ship was well constructed and stable, and our cabin was quite comfortable. Fortunately, I got my sea legs quickly, and I was never bothered by seasickness.

The troops on board were members of an army reserve unit from New Mexico. For many of them, it was their first sea voyage. They were probably going to the Philippines to shore up our defenses. Most of the troops were really not expecting the war to break out anytime soon.

On board ship, Komori and I were told that we had been transferred from the Hawaiian Detachment, U.S. Army, to the Philippine Department, U.S. Army, and assigned to G2. We learned that G2 is one of the staff agencies within the army command: G1 was personnel, G2 intelligence, and G3, transportation. Whenever "2" appeared, it signified intelligence. For example, S2 meant battalion intelligence. Corps of Intelligence Police (CIP), to which we were both assigned, was under G2. The CIP was formed to collect intelligence during the Civil War under President Lincoln. It seemed rather curious that we were already on assignment and were just being told who we belonged to and what we stood for.

We were under strict orders not to fraternize with anyone on board ship except the crew members. The only person aware of our presence and our status was the captain of the *Republic*. Our cabin was located with the officers and the top enlisted personnel. We did not wear uniforms, and our cover story was that we were ship's hands who were slated to join the crew after we got to Manila. Throughout the entire voyage we stayed with the crew, ate in its mess, and otherwise avoided all contact with anyone else.

Early in the trip, I met O'Neill, a friendly man in his fifties who ran the ship's printing shop. His primary duty was to print a daily menu for the officer's mess. I went to his shop each day, just to while away some time and talk with him. Having little else to do, I volunteered to help him with his chores. He taught me to set type and run the machines. We became fast friends and it made time go faster on board ship.

On the second day out of Honolulu, I was sitting out on a deck chair when an officer sat down next to me. As I sat reading, he whispered out of the side of his mouth that I was not supposed to be sitting out there. For the first time, I became aware that I was being watched. From that point on, I exercised greater caution and stuck closer to the crew members on the main deck. We were told that if anyone questioned our status, we should say that we were future crew members and our job assignment would be made by the captain after we got to Manila.

On the fifteenth day out to sea, as the *Republic* got to within three miles of Manila Harbor, Komori and I were abruptly summoned to the bridge of the ship where we found a middle-aged man clad in a white suit who identified himself as Major Nelson W. Raymond, the operations officer for G2, Headquarters, U.S. Army, Philippine Department.

He handed each of us an envelope and said, "Detailed instructions are contained in there. First of all, we will get you off this ship without going through normal landing procedures since we don't want the Philippine commonwealth government officials to identify you. You can read your instructions later en route to your destination. I will drop you off at an appropriate place where you can pick up a taxicab to a hotel that has been designated for you. Be sure to catch a Yellow Cab and as an added precaution, do not refer to street maps in public places since that would arouse the suspicion of the Filipinos."

When the *Republic* finally docked at U.S. Army Pier #1, we were whisked into a waiting cab driven by a special agent. We pulled out of the the area of the pier and as we proceeded down Dewey Boulevard, we read our instructions. I was to go to the Nishikawa Hotel and ask for room and board arrangements. Komori's destination was the Toyo Hotel.

My cover story was that I had just arrived in Manila as a crew member of an American freighter and that I had jumped ship to look for a job in the city. I was also supposed to familiarize myself with the city in the next two days and to be ready for an evening contact meeting with Major Raymond on 23 April 8:00 P.M. I was to walk by City Hall where the pickup would be made.

It was midsummer by the time we got to the Philippines and although I had worn a light-weight suit, I was soaking with perspiration by the time I got to the front desk of the Nishikawa Hotel. The hotel was owned and operated by an affluent Japanese family.

The Nishikawa Hotel was two stories high with twenty-five rooms. It was not a luxurious hotel by any means but it was comfortable, and, best of all, it was centrally located. Breakfast and dinner were included in the room charge for a reason. The hotel catered to Japanese businessmen posted in Manila without their families, and the availability of a Japanese kitchen staff was a boon to life away from home for those men. The owner, Kumataro Fujii, was a well-known and respected Japanese businessman himself and was a frequenter of the Wack Wack Golf Course, where he played golf with noted visitors from Japan.

The hotel management was not well disposed to surprises. My sudden appearance, without advanced reservation, caused a bit of consternation at the front desk. There were many questions, but I stuck by my cover story. They finally relented and gave me a room.

The first few nights were miserable. I was in a strange land, homesick, and uncomfortable in the role of being someone other than myself. The loneliness of it all nearly drove me to tears.

The lizards that scurried across the walls with their annoying nighttime sounds made things even worse. At first, I regarded them as nuisances but as I lay there thinking, it suddenly dawned upon me that the lizard was but a metaphor—like me it was an uninvited guest just one swat away from being thrown out. I left them alone.

It shook me into the realization that I had a mission to perform and it was time to establish my bona fides.

The curiosity of the hotel tenants was naturally aroused by my arrival. They had heard of the *niseis* but they had never come face to face with one. Since all the tenants were unaccompanied family men and therefore reduced to virtual bachelorhood, they all congregated in the small hotel lounge each evening to talk about the day's activities. During the first week, I spent the evenings in my room, unsure of my bearings in a strange land, thinking about the carefree days spent in the company of my friends in Hawaii. I kept wondering how and why I let myself get into this predicament. After a while, even the sound of the lizards reminded me of Hawaii. Moreover, there was not even a radio to fill the void.

Finally I felt comfortable enough to join the group in the hotel lounge. The hotel tenants appeared to range in age from the mid-thirties to midfifties. I was quite junior to them. They all seemed very cordial but at the same time, it was obvious that they were curious—they asked about my age and then they wanted to know what brought me to the Philippines.

I launched into my story about getting tired of island living and wanting to see the world. I said that when the opportunity to work as a crew member on a ship presented itself, I had taken it. When we arrived in Manila, I noticed that the climate and environment here were similar to Hawaii, which prompted me to jump ship. My plan was to find work in Manila until I could continue my travels. The final point that I got across to them was that I was trying to avoid being drafted into the U.S. Army.

They questioned me about family and upbringing. I confided a mixture of fact and fantasy: my parents were from Hiroshima, my father passed away when I was seven years old, and my mother had raised my two sisters, my brother, and I (the youngest). I described the hardships endured by my mother to raise us, and how reluctant she had been to allow me to leave home until she realized that I would be drafted into the U.S. Army. At that point I knew I had won their sympathy. They felt particularly sorry for my mother, widowed and living thousands of miles away from Japan. They promised to care for me like a kid brother and see that I returned safely to my family someday. When I returned to my room that night, my depression of earlier in the evening had diminished.

Thereafter, the tenants made it a point to take me out with them—to cabarets, night clubs, and jai alai matches, and for late-night snacks around town. Their generosity broke the ice and made it possible for me to find my way around town sooner that it could have otherwise.

The night clubs in Manila were lavish, extravagant places of entertainment. The decor was luxurious and the staffs were trained to high levels of efficiency. The cuisine was superb and the wine cellars were stocked with vintage selections. Many night clubs boasted top-flight orchestras and dance floors, and their hostesses were stunning Filipinos and *Mestizos* (Spanish-Filipinos). Drinks were available virtually at the snap of a finger, but since I imbibed very little back then, I usually planted myself near the gaming tables to watch the fast and heavy betting. For myself, I stuck to small wagers at the roulette tables and the slot machines.

Jai alai was a popular, fast-paced game somewhat like handball. It was played with a basketlike racquet fastened to the arms of the players. It was a popular pastime in Manila and among the hotel residents. And, of course, I enjoyed the late-night snacks after the matches. We went out to Chinese restaurants for noodles practically every night of the week.

Among the hotel residents, three were particularly memorable. One was a bank manager and two were importers. Thanks to them, I was able to get acclimated to the hotel and city very quickly. They were genuinely kind and generous to me and I regretted that we had to be friends under such circumstances. I would like to have repaid them after the war, but I never ran into them again.

At exactly 8:00 P.M., on the evening of 23 April 1941, I had my first evening contact with Major Raymond. As arranged, the pickup was made near City Hall and from there, I was driven to Fort Santiago where G2 headquarters were located. The office was a part of a historic landmark. It was the room in which Jose Rizal was imprisoned by the Spaniards following his capture during the rebellion against Spain.

That evening, I was introduced to Col. J. K. Evans, the head of

G2, and Capt. Raymond Beebe, the G2 finance officer. I was told that as a special agent, my badge number would be "B-16" and my code name would be "Sixto Borja." As an undercover agent within the Japanese community of Manila, I would be receiving my instructions and sending reports through a postal mail drop. I was forbidden to have anything associated with the U.S. military in my personal possession. It was arranged by Major Raymond that I would work for the Marsman Trading Company, which represented Sears & Roebuck in the Philippines. My job was to handle the merchandise complaints for Sears as a Marsman employee. Under that guise, my primary responsibility was to observe and identify any Japanese nationals suspected of working for Japanese military intelligence in the Manila area.

Manila was well deserving of the title "Pearl of the Orient." I remember marveling at the scenery when I first drove on Dewey Boulevard. Approaching the city for the first time, one could detect remnants of the ramparts, parapets, and churches that once marked an ancient walled city. The city had a river coursing through it, flanked by magnificent parks, bridges, and new government buildings. The ocean drive was stunning, lined with homes of wealthy and powerful families, which were set well back from the highway and surrounded by verdant stretches of garden and greenery. The landscaping encouraged the best of the tropical trees and shrubs common to the city. The heart of the city was dominated by the High Commissioner's Palace, the Army-Navy Club, elegant apartment complexes, rows of specialty shops, and the famous Manila Hotel, which faced the bay, fronted by palm trees, tropical vines, and flowering plants and trees like those of Hawaii. Manila was a modern and bustling city in every sense.

The Marsman Trading Company was located on Escola Street, right in the heart of Manila. Every morning, I left the hotel between 7:30 and 8:00 A.M. and headed for the Marsman office via the Central Post Office where I checked my mail box for instructions.

I would enter the Marsman office by 8:30 A.M. and spend a few moments chatting with the manager to allay suspicion, just in case I was under surveillance. Then I would leave the store through the back door to head for a nearby movie theater to watch whatever was showing that day. I usually stayed in the theater until noon. Since all stores closed between noon and 2:00 P.M., I usually returned to the hotel at noon, and then made a pretense of going back to work later in the afternoon.

My lifestyle in Manila was comfortable despite my original fears. When I was first told that my base pay as a sergeant would be $80.00 a month, I was incensed because it was half of what I was earning at my last job. However, I found that I was entitled to fringe benefits. As an enlisted man, I received an additional $2.57 a day for food, I was given a clothing allowance, and I was also reimbursed for all operational expenses.

The exchange rate for pesos in relation to dollars was 2:1 and, in those days, laborers were paid a peso a day or $.50 for eight hours of work. Everything was cheap. Cigarettes were a nickel a pack compared to a quarter in Hawaii.

With a clothing allowance of $150.00, I purchased some civilian clothes, including tailor-made white suits, made of both linen and duck cloth. Irish linen suits, tailor-made, cost thirteen pesos or $6.50 U.S. For the first time in my life, I had too much money to spend, or it seemed that way to me. I had never had such a large wardrobe. I was initially puzzled by the instructions passed on to me to spend my allowance only for outer garments, not for undergarments. I understand this is an army regulation that still stands today, but at that time, it was new to me. I tried to return some of the money, but to my surprise, I was ordered to spend the entire allotment. So I made additional purchases. I bought Florsheim shoes at $5.00 a pair, and I indulged myself by purchasing plastic belts and raincoats that were just coming into vogue. It appeared that I was always shopping, and word soon got around about my seemingly extravagant spending habits, leading the manager of the Heacock Store Men's Department to speculate that I was the son of a rich plantation owner in Hawaii. The manager was eager to show me all of the store's new shipments, and with my generous allowance, I was a willing shopper. My last purchase was a beautiful suede jacket that I bought for $42.50. Under normal circumstances, it would have been far too extravagant for me.

In the steamy summer heat of Manila, I went through about three suits a day. Fortunately, laundry was cheap, and for $2.00 a month, I hired a maid to take care of all of my hand laundry.

Each day I had to keep out of sight. Sometimes I went to movies, but when I ran out of movies to see, I took train rides out to the countryside. It was a good way to explore some of the outlying areas and to enjoy some peace and quiet. Usually, I would get food from one of the many Chinese stores and then walk from place to place.

I could not afford to walk around too much, however, lest I arouse the suspicion of the local residents. They were apt to wonder why a Japanese was regularly roaming the countryside.

There were about two thousand Japanese nationals residing in and around Manila. They were mostly merchants who ran department stores and shops in the city. The Japanese presence in the Philippines was led by businessmen and entrepreneurs who arrived prior to World War I. The first group went to Mindanao to engage in the cultivation of hemp. The oldest Japanese firm in the Philippines, I was told, was Furukawa Kogyo. The Japanese also went into mining for gold and silver in Luzon. Japanese filled the managerial and entrepreneurial ranks. There were no Japanese laborers. This task was left to the Filipinos.

Other groups made Manila their home. The large Chinese population resided mostly in the Chinatown area, close to their shops, restaurants, and temples. Many of the Americans there were U.S. corporate representatives and others were affiliated with the High Commissioner's Office. In addition, there was a huge American military community. Filipinos were found in all occupations, but the wealthiest seemed to be concentrated in the professions. They were the bankers, lawyers, doctors, and dentists who prospered in the thriving prewar economy.

The Filipinos had been promised independence in 1948 by the United States. They were aware of its coming, but there seemed to be few preparations for moving in that direction. When the war broke out, the issue of independence was quickly superseded by a more fundamental concern for survival.

Prior to the outbreak of the war, the Filipino people were very friendly to Americans. They also got along very well with the Japanese, particularly those who had provided them with long years of sustenance and employment. In the opinion of many Western businessmen in Manila, before World War II, the Japanese were better established and welcomed in the Philippines than anyone else. However, any goodwill they enjoyed quickly evaporated with the outbreak of the war.

As the summer of 1941 approached, there was a feeling in the Japanese community that war would come, but not right away. America was still at peace but within the year, Denmark, Norway, Holland, Belgium, and France had all been overwhelmed by Nazi Germany. The Battle of Britain was underway and the German invasion of Russia made it increasingly unlikely that war could be avoided.

Things were also turning ominous in the Pacific. Japan had signed the Tripartite Pact with Germany and Italy and had proceeded to take French Indochina. The Americans responded with an embargo on Japan's oil supply, which cut into its war effort in China and threatened its industrial production.

Within the Japanese community in Manila, the situation did indeed look serious to some but few showed any signs of alarm. The consensus was that the diplomatic talks going on between the United States and Japan would somehow prevent fighting from breaking out. Preliminary negotiations with the United States began under the helm of the Japanese ambassador to the United States, Kichisaburo Nomura, who was replaced by Ambassador Saburo Kurusu when the Tojo cabinet was established in the fall of 1941. In fact, a bit of optimism was heard in Manila when it became known that Ambassador Kurusu would join in the negotiations. Kurusu routed his flight through Manila on his way to Washington, and somehow it was felt that Kurusu, who was quite knowledgeable about the West, would be able to pull off the negotiations successfully. The U.S. military establishment in the Philippines was much more alert to the signs, however, and began preparations for the defense of the islands.

During this time, Major Raymond briefed me about Clarence Yamagata, a Japanese-American practicing law in Manila. He was also employed by the Japanese embassy in Manila as a legal advisor. He handled most of the legal matters for the embassy. Because of his language capabilities in both English and Japanese and his legal training in America, he was uniquely qualified to be the legal counsel in Manila. The major wanted me to find out more about him.

One day, I called on him at his office without making an appointment. He seemed somewhat taken aback at first, so I said, "Hi, I'm Dick Sakakida and I'm from Hawaii too." I said I had heard about him at the Nishikawa Hotel. The minute he realized that I was from Hawaii, he opened up to me as most Hawaiians are likely to do whenever they meet a fellow Hawaiian in a foreign land. But I could tell that he was still wary of my intentions. His office was located on Escolia Street near the Heacock Department Store, which I frequented almost every day at lunchtime. We talked at length about our Hawaiian connections and he steered clear of anything having to do with U.S.-Japanese relations. Since it was our first meeting, I scrupulously avoided the subject myself.

As relations between the United States and Japan worsened, the United States froze all of the assets of Japanese citizens in the Philippines. When the order went into effect, all Japanese residents in Manila were required to file asset reports with the U.S. High Commissioner's Office. Suddenly, the demand for Clarence's services escalated. The Japanese found him to be just the man to assist them in filling out the required forms.

Clarence was soon swamped with requests and he suggested that I help him by moonlighting after work. "You can work out of your hotel room. It's a convenient place to get to," he said. I accepted, but not for monetary gain. Instead, I saw it as an opportune way to expand my contacts within the Japanese community. Major Raymond at G2 heartily endorsed the idea. What intrigued him was a question in the form that asked about prior military service of those filling out the forms. I worked out of my hotel room and did not charge for my services. This brought dozens of Japanese to my room every night, all seeking assistance with their forms. In the process, I discovered that about 50 percent of the Japanese males in Manila were Japanese military reservists.

I also discovered that the principal of a Japanese-language school, who had long been suspected by U.S. military intelligence of being a "sleeper" agent, was indeed a major in the reserves. When we got to the part about military service, he was reluctant to reply and he nervously inquired what would happen if he replied negatively. I tried to muster as much sympathy as I could to allay his suspicion and then I asked him why. "I am the ranking army officer in the Japanese Reserve Corps in the Philippines," he replied. He then gave me a rambling account of his military background, and how he was assigned to military intelligence. In order to assure his confidence in me, I suggested that he take a chance by answering the question negatively. He was obviously relieved by my suggestion. Of course, I did send a report on him to Major Raymond next morning.

Japanese intelligence was well prepared for the invasion of the Philippines and their best sources of information were established by the Japanese Navy. Men from the navy were well established in a network that existed long before the outbreak of hostilities. The reliance on naval personnel was due to a long tradition of travel and training abroad, particularly in training cruises, which made them more cosmopolitan in their outlook and better prepared to handle themselves in foreign countries and cultures.

Japanese intelligence agents trained at the Nakano Intelligence School. Its students were elite candidates and selection for training in the service was considered a rare honor. The security checks were stringent and those making the final selection lists were generally officers. Once selected, the person's name was stricken from his family register and he was declared officially "dead." The agent would then be given a new identity before being dispatched to a foreign country. Many families were reportedly led to believe that their sons had been killed in action. Once inducted into the intelligence service, agents were not allowed to communicate with their families. Following World War II, many agents who had been presumed dead managed to return home, much to the surprise of families and friends.

The tradition of intelligence was well established in Japan and the work of Japanese Military Intelligence in the Philippines was outstanding. They had superbly detailed maps and layouts of the labyrinth of tunnels that the United States had built at Corregidor. They knew the location of every coastal artillery battery, and they had in their possession a detailed description of our weapons and firepower. The maps were superior to our own maps and yet it was we and not they who had built and fortified Corregidor.

In addition to the Japanese school principal, a Japanese banker in Manila was suspected of being an intelligence agent. He was unlike any other ordinary banker in his dress, speech, and conduct. His unusual manner of walking led me to suspect him: he always kept his left hand straight along the seam of his trousers while allowing his right arm to swing freely on the other side. This was the walk of officers who spent many years holding the scabbard of their sabers with their left hand while walking or parading. While filling out his form, he confided to me that he was a naval officer on active duty, unbeknownst even to members of his own staff at the bank. His primary mission in Manila was to report on the economy of the Philippines. Again, I made a special exception for him on the form, which I promptly reported to Major Raymond at G2.

When Clarence heard that I was assisting the Japanese community without charge, he seemed impressed and decided to find me a job with the Japanese embassy. He wanted to find me a job with better pay and higher social standing. His contact in the Japanese Embassy also happened to be born and raised in Hawaii but had renounced his American citizenship to enter the Japanese Foreign Service. Through Clarence, I was offered a position at the Japanese consulate in Mindanao. I passed the news of the offer to Major Raymond who was quite taken by the idea. Since war between the United States and Japan seemed imminent, G2 thought it would be beneficial to have a man inside the consulate with possible access to classified information. I conveyed my interest in the job through Clarence and I was advised that a position would become available in January 1942. Unfortunately, the outbreak of war on 7 December 1941 put an end to that idea.

Life as a special agent had taken a drastic turn for me. Relations between the United States and Japan had worsened considerably. When Japanese embassy personnel began the evacuation of dependents, I suddenly realized that we were drawing close to war in Manila. In late November, the Japanese ship *Nitta Maru* was sent to Manila to pick up families returning to Japan. Among the evacuees were members of Clarence's family, but even though I was still in regular contact with Clarence, he had never mentioned to me that his family was being urged to return to Japan. The fact that there was a flurry of activity under a cloak of official silence convinced me even more that things were rapidly coming to a head between the United States and Japan.

Meanwhile, I was about to be surprised by an event that would provide a welcome distraction from the depressing thoughts of war. The proprietor of the Nishikawa Hotel and his wife had made me feel quite at home from the beginning. Their generosity and kindness had freed me of the loneliness and alienation of my first days in Manila, and, more importantly, it ingratiated me with the rest of the people from Japan and the hotel staff.

I settled into a comfortable relationship with Mr. and Mrs. Fujii. They were impressed by my Buddhist observation of *meinichi*, or Commemoration Day—the anniversay of my father's death. On such occasions, no meat is consumed during the evening meal or at breakfast the next morning. They were apparently quite taken by the observance of such an old tradition by a young Japanese-American. On 19 November the couple surprised me with a sumptuous birthday dinner for my twenty-first birthday to which all of the permanent residents at the hotel were invited. At the party, they revealed that my mother had requested the party secretly, and they told me how impressed they were with my filial devotion; they further announced they wanted to ask my mother whether they could adopt me as their heir. I would inherit all of their possessions in Tokyo and Manila.

I was stunned by the revelation. At the same time, I was quite surprised and, frankly, very flattered to learn of their genuine affection and regard for me. It never dawned on me that I was being observed so closely. The only thing that I was aware of was the warmth and spontaneity that marked our relationship.

The adoption proposal, of course, was out of the question. My mother would never have agreed. Mrs. Fujii said that she was sure that would be my mother's reaction but she wanted to forward the proposal anyway. Nevertheless, the birthday party was a pleasant surprise and the last happy interlude before all hell broke loose.

On 27 November 1941, Major Raymond told me that all U.S. military forces in the Philippines had gone on full alert. In the event of any hostilities, I was to continue my surveillance of the Japanese community, and, if possible, I was to enter an evacuation camp with the rest of the Japanese. At the appropriate time, Raymond would arrange to have me picked up by U.S. authorities. He wanted me to be with the Japanese community as long as possible to report on anything that would be of interest to G2.

So my fate was to remain under cover even in the event of a shooting war. I didn't have very long to wait.

Chapter 5

OUTBREAK OF WAR

According to Gen. Jonathan Wainwright, the plan for the defense of the Philippines was originally conceived as part of a theoretical exercise designed for students at the U.S. Army War College and the command and general staff schools.

In a book published after the war, he recalled that

> War Plan Orange-3, a variation of a plan about twenty years old was this: in the event of a successful Japanese landing on the main island of Luzon, the Philippine Division and the Philippine Army, if unable to beat off the landings and subsequent advance of the theoretical enemy, were to fight delaying actions and withdraw into Bataan Peninsula. The plan envisioned a six-month stand on Bataan, by which time aid from the United States would arrive.

He added that "MacArthur and I agreed that it was a defeatist plan but our feeling in the matter did not change it."

My own view was that of a foot soldier but as subsequent events were to bear out, we were woefully unprepared for the Japanese invasion of the Philippines. The U.S. Command in the Philippines had neither the time nor the resources to mount the kind of all-out preparations that were required to confront the seasoned and well-organized Japanese task force.

The last major engineering projects to fortify the islands occurred in 1914 when Fort Mills, Fort Hughes, Fort Drum, and Fort Frank were transformed into what was then called "The Gibraltar of the East." By 1914 standards, the title was well deserved. It was a formidable defensive network capable of withstanding attacks from the sea and of destroying any enemy ship daring to pass into Manila Bay. But, aided by outstanding intelligence reporting in 1941, the Japanese struck through the air and otherwise skirted those defensive strongholds in plotting their troop landings.

Our one source of superiority was the much heralded squadron of B-17s that came to the Philippines prior to the Japanese invasion to bolster our defenses. Unfortunately, most of our air strength was destroyed in a swift air raid conducted on Clark Field by a large force of Japanese bombers and fighter planes on 8 December 1941. However, beyond the B-17s and some P-40s, we had obsolete planes such as the B-18 and Martin B-10 bombers and the Republic P-35 and Boeing P-26 fighters, which were no match for what the Japanese possessed.

When the air raids first began at Clark Field, we were too far removed as residents of Manila to understand what was going on out there. In fact, 8 December 1941, the day of the first air strike on Clark Field, fell on a Monday and things started out like any other day at the Nishikawa Hotel. I got up at the usual time, went down for breakfast at the hotel dining room, and then headed for the post office to check for messages at the mail drop.

As I neared the post office building, I heard the newsboys on the street hawking their papers with their usual come-on, "Extra! Extra! Read all about it!" Figuring that this was just another local matter that papers habitually sensationalized to boost circulation, I didn't pay much attention. As I got closer, however, I could see a headline, "PEARL HARBOR BOMBED!" Pearl Harbor was near my home and family. I grabbed a newspaper and read with astonishment about the surprise Japanese attack the previous day. Surely, I thought, the United States was now at war with Japan.

I had no message in my mail drop. Instead of going to the Marsman Company office as I did every day, I went right back to the Nishikawa Hotel, where pandemonium reigned.

The Japanese residents were as shocked as I was. Commotion filled the hotel lobby. Most of the people that I ran into seemed at a loss, and some showed genuine despair. Everything happened too suddenly for them, even though they had been aware of the possibility that war would break out. They were ordinary citizens, to whom war always comes as a shock. Today they felt as I did: we were pawns in events over which we had no control. At least, I was better prepared than they were.

Amid the turmoil, I rushed up to my room to prepare for any emergency contingency. I quickly packed a bag of necessities—shirts, trousers, underwear, socks, an extra pair of shoes, toiletries—just in case I had to leave on short notice.

As ordered by Major Raymond, in the event of the outbreak of war, my first responsibility was to stay with the Japanese community, so it was important for me to position myself for any kind of move. I went back down to the lobby to see what was happening. I felt quite insecure. Like the rest of the people in the hotel, I was fearful and worried because of the uncertainty of the moment. Being under cover made me tense and guarded anyway, but now we were at war. It was a brand new ball game and I prayed that my cover would remain intact.

There was a similarity between my situation and that of the Japanese around me. They were foreigners in a far-off land where life had been good and the people friendly. Now, all of a sudden, they were unwelcome foreigners in hostile territory. In the Japanese enclave, I was only one slip away from being in the same boat. But in my case, I would be under Japanese persecution. It is easy enough to talk about war but it is another matter to suddenly come face to face with it. No one, least of all the army, had prepared me for this. I was just thrown into the fray and I was thankful that I had the wit and moxie that I learned on the streets of Palama to help me keep my cool. This was a time when street smarts counted far more than any lessons in training manuals.

When I arrived back in the lobby, I could see the proprietor of the hotel on the telephone, looking very serious and nodding with every reply. He was not his usual self, smiling and speaking graciously to guests calling into the hotel. I could tell that something was up and that we would know about it very quickly.

I was right. As soon as he hung up, he turned to address the hotel residents who had by then congregated into small groups and were too immersed in animated conversation to notice that he wanted their attention. Anxiety was causing everyone to act very un-Japanese. The reticence had disappeared from their behavior, but somehow that was reassuring—it made them seem like the rest of us. But as his repeated plea for attention began to resonate more forcefully through the lobby, the noise faded into total silence. A sense of relief settled over us as a semblance of order was finally restored.

Mustering calm and composure, he announced, "I have just finished talking to a representative of the Japanese Association of Manila. He has been in contact with the Philippine Constabulary to arrange for the evacuation of all Japanese nationals in Manila to the Nippon Club on Taft Avenue. Our orders are to evacuate these premises immediately. I would advise all of you to comply fully with this order while it is possible to do so under the protection of the Philippine Constabulary. At this point, none of us knows what the future holds. Pack only what is needed to meet your basic everyday needs. At some time in the future, we will try to arrange to return to the hotel to retrieve the rest of your possessions. Please pack your bags now and prepare to leave immediately."

This time, everyone returned to their rooms in silence. They were no longer uncertain about what to do.

The evacuation of the hotel proceeded very smoothly. Waiting buses transported the people and trucks hauled their bags and other paraphernalia.

The hotel owner asked me if I would drive him and his wife to the Nippon Club in his own vehicle, which I was happy to do under the circumstance. I had driven his car on many other occasions, and since we were on such cordial terms, it did not seem unusual at all for me to drive for them.

I was apprehensive about getting into the Nippon Club. There were bound to be questions regardless of whether the officials doing the security screening were American or Japanese. At the same time,

I was curious to see what the club was like inside. I had passed by it on a number of occasions but I had never been on the premises.

The Nippon Club was a Japanese businessmen's club and was a modern equivalent of the chamber of commerce. It was a huge two-story wooden building and in many respects, it was like many of the country club buildings of the past. There was no golf course, but it had tennis courts and a huge expanse of well-kept lawn where other recreational games were played. It also had a restaurant, snack facilities, meeting rooms, and a spacious hall that could hold large conferences, parties, or even dances.

When I drove up the driveway, the place was already teeming with people. I double-parked in front of the club to let my passengers off first. I helped them with their bags and told them to check into the club while I parked the car. After parking in the club lot, I retrieved my own bag from the trunk and headed toward the building.

When I got to the registration desk, the constabulary members were checking all baggage items. A couple of agents in civilian clothes were also there with the members of the Filipino Constabulary Force. One of them began looking through my things. When he saw my American passport, he did a double take.

At that time, we did not know each other but I learned later that he was Paul Marinas, an agent of G2. "Hey," he said, "you're an American citizen. This place is only for the Japanese and you don't belong here." At that point, I was not too worried about my cover because a lot of the people checking into the Nippon Club knew me. What worried me was that I would be kept out of the club and thus prevented from following my orders. And there I was, being threatened by a man from G2 itself.

"Look," I pleaded, "you can see that I look Japanese. We're at war and the Filipinos outside this compound are not going to stop me and ask me about my citizenship. As far as they are concerned, I'm a *Happon* (Japanese), and I'm liable to get shot."

He thought about what I said for a moment and relented. "All right," he said, "but remember, you are entering voluntarily, and you're free to leave anytime you wish." He immediately contacted

71

the officer in charge of the constabulary unit, who promised me an escort for safety if I should decide to leave.

With that reassurance and a sigh of relief, I finally entered the club. Because of the large number of people, it was impossible to accommodate everyone inside the building. So women and children were settled indoors and the men made their beds outdoors.

We were each issued a blanket for sleeping gear. I wanted to remain anonymous and was aided in this desire by the huge influx of people, many of whom did not know each other. Social distinctions were very pronounced among the Japanese so there was no immediate rush to establish new relationships. The people I knew from the Nishikawa Hotel treated me as usual, so there were few questions asked. Besides, from the very beginning, a kind of siege mentality had set in, which drew us all together in a common dilemma.

I also made it a point to see that the hotel owner and his wife were all right. If anything happened to me, I needed all the help I could get and I knew that I could rely on them.

In the excitement, I had forgotten about eating and was starting to get very hungry. Our food was served in a hall inside the clubhouse. I ventured in for my first meal and found people making their way around buffet tables. The food was simple Japanese fare with lots of basic rice balls. I ate just enough to cut my hunger and went searching for a place to sleep that night.

I finally chose the tennis court. It was hard but level, fenced, and guarded by heavy shrubs. At least the fence provided a modicum of privacy, meaning that I wasn't completely surrounded by other bodies.

The rest of the day was uneventful, but the long hours of idleness left too much time to worry. It was then that I succumbed to the lure of cigarettes. I bought a pack of Camels and smoked every one.

On day two, the lieutenant in charge of the platoon of Filipino guards called me to his post. He had apparently been briefed further by the American command because he too assured me of my freedom of movement. I was extremely grateful for the reassurance.

Since I was free to go and the routine was becoming boring, I ventured out to the Heacock Department Store, which had a restaurant that I had regularly patronized in the past. I could get American food and work off my nervous energy.

On the third day as I was preparing to go out, a Nippon Club officer asked me to pick up some milk and other perishable food for the people in the compound. The children, in particular, had needs that could not be met at the club. I took this as a golden opportunity to ingratiate myself with Nippon Club authorities and quickly agreed to help.

The constabulary lent two men to assist me, so I borrowed the hotel owner's car and drove to the Philippine Cold Storage in Quiapo. We loaded the car with every refrigerated item that we could find there.

On the way back, I decided to stop off at the Nishikawa Hotel to pick up more of my personal belongings. With two members of the Philippine Constabulary escorting me, I was confident that nothing would go amiss. I was wrong.

There was an eerie quiet about the hotel when we got there. Inside, we discovered that the place had been ransacked. My room was a mess and everything of any value had been stolen. I had a sudden urge to vacate the premises. I felt as if we were being watched.

"Let's get out of here," I said to my companions. They too seemed eager to leave.

Just as we were walking out, we heard someone say, "Hold it, where you are!" We all froze in place.

We were suddenly surrounded by four counterintelligence agents from the Philippine Constabulary who entered with guns drawn.

"Who are you?" one of them asked.

"My name is Richard Sakakida. I am an American and these two men are members of the Philippine Constabulary who have been detailed to accompany me on an errand in town," I replied.

"What are you doing in this hotel?" he continued.

"I came back to pick up some personal belongings but I found my room ransacked so I was just about to leave," I explained.

"Liar!" he screamed. "You must be a Japanese spy and these two men are imposters posing as members of the constabulary."

73

"You're wrong, sir," the two men with me replied, but they were quickly silenced. "I'll get to you two in due time," he told them.

"Where are you residing now?" he asked as he turned back to me.

"The Nippon Club," I said.

"Aha, if you are an American as you claim, what are you doing there? That's supposed to be for Japanese nationals only. Don't you know that?" he continued with increased relish.

"I don't know. I was at the Nishikawa Hotel and I was sent there like everyone else at the hotel. Since I look Japanese, they must have sent me there regardless. They may also have done that for my own safety. You can see these men were sent out with me to protect me."

He glared contemptuously at my companions, still convinced that they were Japanese sympathizers in constabulary uniforms. Nothing I said made a difference. I was arrested, handcuffed, jerked around, and taken to the Philippine Constabulary Headquarters. When we got to headquarters, they dragged me into the counterintelligence commander's office. The charge was that I was a Japanese spy at large, running around town with two pro-Japanese Filipinos masquerading as constabulary personnel.

The commander, who obviously saw me as a real quarry, was relentless in his questioning. He was determined to implicate me and if need be, break me. I stuck to my old cover story. This time, it was not the Japanese questioning me, it was the Filipinos. The commander and his coterie of interrogators remained firmly unconvinced. They insisted that I was a Japanese spy. But this test of my credibility simply made me more determined to hold my ground. As the questions continued, the interrogators became increasingly testy in their remarks. I found myself bristling with anger with each exchange.

At one point, another agent entered the room to consult with the commander. As he passed by, he looked at me and seemed startled. He retreated back to the commander and whispered into his ear. The commander's demeanor immediately changed from utter contempt to total forgiveness.

"Young man," he said as he turned to me. "You should have told me at the outset that you are a member of G2, U.S. Army, and we wouldn't have had to go through all of this." The moment he said that, my mind flashed back to an incident that occurred soon after I arrived in the Philippines.

One day, I accompanied Mr. Shimada, a Nishikawa resident, to the Sumitomo Bank. As we came around the corner of the bank building, someone stepped hard on my foot. The man muttered an apology and walked off. I let the matter pass while I tended to my foot, which was still smarting with pain. Then I realized that I was the victim of a well-executed ruse. In that moment of distraction, a pickpocket had made off with my wallet. The wallet contained my identification card, my passport, and a hundred pesos. I immediately called Major Raymond about the incident.

"You were a victim of a pickpocket gang," he told me. "Those gangs are common in Manila. Don't expect your wallet to be returned. In the meantime, I'll have another passport issued to you."

It was a most disappointing and frustrating day for me, and I hated to admit that I had been victimized. But it was a valuable lesson. Mr. Shimada, who witnessed the entire incident, offered to make up the money that I had lost but I, of course, refused.

I spent the rest of the afternoon sulking in my hotel room and otherwise getting down on myself for being caught flat-footed. But like every rookie, I had to learn the hard way. As I lay in bed, staring at the bare ceiling, there was a knock on my door. "Come in," I said. It was the yard man employed by the hotel.

"I found this thrown over the fence on the side lawn," he said. He held up my wallet.

I bolted out of bed and examined the wallet. Much to my surprise, nothing was missing, not even a single peso. I thanked the yard man and tipped him generously for bringing the wallet up to my room.

I was immediately suspicious. There was something very strange about having my wallet stolen and then having it thrown into the hotel yard a few hours later with everything intact. I again called Major Raymond. His comment was, "I guess our friends in the Philippine Constabulary must have been on your tail. We'll find out soon enough."

Apparently the commander of the constabulary didn't know about me, but it was clear one of his agents did. I continued to deny my affiliation with the U.S. Army, just in case, but I heard the commander calling Major Raymond and saying, "Will you come to my office to get Richard Sakakida?"

The atmosphere lightened radically in the musty interrogation room. Though I didn't complain, I was fit to be tied. I resented the way I had been roughed up, and I was worried that my cover may have been compromised so that I would not be able to go back to the Nippon Club. Moreover, all of the milk and other perishable refrigerated products for the children were probably spoiled, stolen, or confiscated by then. And the hotel owner's Pontiac that I had borrowed to go into town was also probably gone. Besides, interrogations are always provocative and I was seething with fury in spite of all the smiles suddenly being visited on me.

Within an hour, Raymond arrived. The Filipino commander was effusive in his greeting and shook the major's hand repeatedly. As they retreated to his office, I could see the commander excitedly explaining what had happened.

As he came out of the office, Major Raymond said, "Gee Richard, I'm sorry this happened." I was fuming but kept silent.

I later filed a complaint with the commander, however, about the way his personnel manhandled me at the Nishikawa Hotel, which I regarded as excessive. The way I was feeling, I was not about to let them off the hook. I don't know how the major felt about my complaint but I was too upset to care.

Back at the hotel, my worst fears were confirmed. Everything was gone—the perishable food, the Pontiac, everything had disappeared. I was sick.

As we drove toward G2 headquarters, I told Major Raymond that something had to be done to resolve the situation. All the food and provisions that I had purchased for the club were gone and so was the car. I knew the people at the Nippon Club would suspect me of stealing their money and the car. Even a hint of suspicion could devastate my credibility within the Japanese community and ruin my cover story at the same time.

The major agreed and quickly came up with a plan. I would be unceremoniously hauled into the Nippon Club by two men in uniform, as if I had been placed under arrest by the U.S. military.

Actually, these two men would be G2 agents dressed in military uniforms.

The two agents played their roles very well. I was taken into the Nippon Club at gunpoint and told not to speak to anyone. I was ordered to get my personal belongings and leave the club. The whole affair was staged for maximum effect, and it was obvious from the faces of the people in the compound that they understood something unfortunate had befallen me and there were uncontrollable reasons underlying the disappearance of the money and the car.

My experience at the Nippon Club affirmed something that I had learned in Hawaii. There is nothing worse than feeling isolated in a small, crowded place. I was or was not Japanese depending on who I was with. To be or not to be was governed by circumstances. It was frustrating, nerve-racking, and painfully private.

I was now destined for an American enclave in the Philippines. I was comfortable with the prospect of redeeming my place in the U.S. military establishment, even though there were bound to be questions about "looking Japanese" and coming in from the cold.

I entered the Nippon Club on 8 December 1941. On that day, a Japanese invasion task force began the shelling of Wake Island. By 10 December, Guam had fallen into Japanese hands and the first Japanese troops were setting foot on Philippine soil. I was completely unaware of those developments. But I would learn about how the war was going soon enough.

Chapter 6

BACK IN THE FOLD

My ouster from the Nippon Club, staged courtesy of G2, left me with just one alternative and that was to return to the fold of the United States Army. For once, it was a welcome alternative. The tensions of the previous week had taken a toll on me and it was nice to be back in a predictable environment.

Yet, from an operational standpoint, I still felt a pang of regret over what I regarded as a premature exit from the club. However, it soon became apparent that my pullout was fortuitous. I never imagined that the advance of the Japanese landing forces on Luzon would be so swift. Under the circumstances, G2 would have had to find some way to extricate me from the Nippon Club anyway.

Up until then, I had felt very comfortable with the reassurances issued by General MacArthur's headquarters and the United States Military Command that the Japanese invasion would be repulsed decisively. The reassurances were important as we faced the unknown. We were still not exposed to the fighting going on north of us and we had no reason to doubt the strength of our defensive network on Luzon. Moreover, an abiding sense of patriotism and pride in America was my defense against negativism, a sentiment that prevailed all around me.

My next abode was Fort Santiago, where G2 was located. To have called the place an abode was a misnomer because there were no separate living quarters to speak of. We simply worked and slept at our desks but we accepted that as a condition of war, something that few of us had experienced before. Most of us were also unaware that being literally hemmed in as we were in our offices was reflective of what was happening to our forces in the northern regions of Luzon.

By 10 December, there was an escalation of Japanese air attacks in the Philippines but the initial raids were directed at U.S. airfields. The purpose of the enemy air attacks was to neutralize U.S. airpower and to achieve air supremacy to support further landing operations in Luzon. Between 10 and 12 December, the Japanese invasion forces landed at six locations: Batan Island, Aparri, Vigan, Legazpi, Davao, and Jolo Island. Being in Manila proper, we had no idea how the war was going. Besides, it had only been about a week since the first air raid on Clark Field.

Our first exposure to a Japanese air raid occurred on 10 December when the port facilities at Cavite were attacked. It was a beautiful day in Manila. It was cool, the sky was clear blue, with hardly a trace of clouds. It was a kind of day that would ordinarily bring out the best attributes of Manila. But instead of a feast for the eyes, we witnessed our first enemy air raid. From our vantage point across the bay in Manila, we could see black smoke billowing into the sky as the bombs exploded around the port, but we were too far away to assess the extent of the damage. But it was a clear sign that it was only a matter of time before the impact of such raids would be felt in Manila.

Soon after, rumors ran rife. Fear and uncertainty had a way of imparting instant credibility to even the most unbelievable stories. For example, we heard the tale of a beautiful woman of Japanese ancestry who, as a trusted employee of the base, somehow aided and abetted the Japanese attack. According to the story, in the aftermath of the attack, a group of American officers at the base drew lots to summarily execute her, and it fell upon a young naval officer who just happened to be in love with the condemned woman to execute her—which he did without any qualms whatsoever. Official investigations revealed that there was no substance to that or other similar stories about a fifth column operating at the base. But in the prevailing climate, anything bearing even a hint of Japanese complicity was suspect. Since I was back in the fold, however, I was not subjected to such threats as a lone Japanese-American.

It was later reported that the entire naval yard at Cavite was set ablaze, resulting in the destruction of the power plant, dispensary, repair shops, warehouses, barracks, and radio station. In one fell swoop, the Asiatic Fleet in the Philippines as well as Cavite was rendered useless.

Overnight, the city of Manila became a mere caricature of beauty and gentility. Once fashionable shops and boutiques, their show windows crisscrossed with tape and entrances walled with sand bags, suddenly added to the pall cast over the once-vibrant downtown area.

There was an immediate run on the banks in Manila and hoarding was rampant throughout the city. Every day, outside our building at Fort Santiago, one could see vehicles of every size, shape, form, and type clogging the roads as people exited the city. Oddly enough, as city residents tried to go out, rural residents came seeking safety in the city. The crush of people, machinery, and animals joined in a common but haphazard attempt at escape added poignancy to the turmoil of the beleagured city. I felt particularly sorry for the Filipino people caught in this war and was grateful that it was not happening in Hawaii or in any American city. The scene was riveting to the point of distraction and as I paused to watch it, I had to remind myself I had work to do.

At Fort Santigo, I was in khaki uniform again and it felt good. The office to which I was assigned was crowded and also pervaded by activity.

On paper, my duties and responsibilities were essentially the same. However, as the crisis worsened, there was no time for fine bureaucratic distinctions about who was supposed to do what. We simply did what needed to be done at any given moment. Because of a shortage of qualified Japanese linguists, my lines of responsibilities ranged from psychological warfare, radio intercepts, cryptology, and prisoner interrogation, to the translation of captured enemy docu-

81

ments. I had been reunited with Arthur Komori, who had also been plucked out of a Japanese enclave, but there were simply not enough of us around to do the critical work of filling in the information gaps.

One of my first duties was to interrogate crew members of the Japanese planes that were downed during the early days of the war. In early December, most of the Japanese bombing raids originated out of Taiwan.

It was a novel experience for me on a number of counts. For the first time, I was doing the questioning. Even though I had suffered being on the other side, it was invaluable to my own understanding of prisoner mentality. I was determined not to lose my prisoners by merely relying on physical and mental coercion. It was a learning experience, since I had never had any formal training in interrogation techniques. For me, it was a seat-of-the-pants approach based on common sense. I had an advantage over the prisoners and I was also armed with a set of G2 requirements on the type of information that was critical to American needs.

The first time the Japanese prisoners were brought into my office, they were dumbfounded to find an Asian among a sea of white faces. Due to my inexperience, it took a while to really connect with the prisoners. I was not about to admit to or even betray any hint of nervousness but I was feeling the pressure. I knew that there was bound to be a difference in the levels of indoctrination between the officers and enlisted men. Fortunately, there were no officers in the first group of prisoners brought to me. I surmised that there would be distinctions between the grizzly veterans and the inexperienced young recruits, particulary those who were not well educated.

The one thing that all of the prisoners shared was their firm belief that it was a disgrace to be captured by the enemy. Death was preferable to capture. With more and more experience, however, I learned to drive the point home to them that in spite of what they were told, they were prisoners and that was what they had to face up to. Having escaped death or been prevented from dying, many were at a loss to figure out what was expected of them under such unforseen circumstances. They had not been trained to handle the contingency of capture under circumstances beyond their control.

I was also aided by the absence of any noncom or officer to rally their resistance. Once I was able to help them distinguish between what they were told to believe and reality, which did not have to reduce their self-image or make them feel disgraced, I was able to connect with them and obtain a great deal of useful information that went well beyond the pro forma tendency to provide only one's name, rank, and serial number. Another ploy that Arthur Komori and I used was to accept what the prisoners said at face value during the first go-around and then check other sources to determine their veracity. Those confronted with their lying in subsequent interrogations often broke down in shame and told us all they knew. Many tried to fool me by relying on pseudonyms. It became a kind of cat-and-mouse game replete with shifting rules and tactics.

I was just starting to get the hang of interrogation and was hopeful of developing a comprehensive method of my own when fate intruded again. There were just too many irons in the fire at G2, each requiring Japanese-language resources that did not exist at sufficient levels to satisfy all of the demands. Moreover, with a full workload occupying us day and night, it was difficult to really stop to find out how the war was going outside of the city. Unbeknownst to many of us, our time in Manila was rapidly coming to a close. I thought I would be at Fort Santiago for a spell, at least for a few months. Instead, my stay at the fort was to be only a matter of days.

Much to my chagrin and that of every other American soldier around me, when the news that the defense of Luzon was going badly came to us, we were stunned. The Japanese landings in northern Luzon were joined by successful Japanese landings at Lingayen Gulf and Lamon Bay on 22 December. On 23 December, General MacArthur ordered a fallback to Bataan, which meant that the fighting would now turn to delaying the Japanese advance until the bulk of U.S. and Philippine troops could be evacuated to the Bataan Peninsula. It also meant that War Plan Orange-3 would be going into effect.

On 24 December 1941, Manila was declared an open city. That very night, Christmas Eve, we were ordered to evacuate Fort Santiago. The U.S. forces went either to Bataan or Corregidor.

One thing that crossed my mind as I prepared to depart was the disposition of the Japanese prisoners. There was no way that they could be taken along. They were to be left in place in our prisons, and I wondered whether our paths would cross again, and especially if questions about my cover would ever emerge.

Nevertheless, I set about destroying our classified files and anything else considered vital to our security. That night, I boarded the USS *Panay* with hundreds of other American troops. The USS *Panay* was a vessel that had plied the waters around the Philippines as an interisland steamer. Our group was temporarily assigned to Middleside, Corregidor, and the nighttime trip on the crowded steamer took approximately two hours. Fortunately, there were no untoward incidents along the way. The next day was like any other day in the evacuation, but it shouldn't have been, because it was Christmas Day. There were no hot meals, just cold rations to mark a cold turn in our lives.

At Corregidor, I was placed under the supervision of Col. Stuart Wood, a language officer who was trained in Japan and assigned to the Philippines directly from Tokyo. It was encouraging to find an American officer with a Japanese-language capability as well as a basic understanding of Japanese culture and psychology. It was always much easier to communicate with someone with his background about operational matters, particularly since few of our soldiers were trained to understand the enemy.

When we got to Corregidor, our confidence was buoyed by the presence of a feisty and supremely confident group of U.S. Marines who had been evacuated to Corregidor from Shanghai, China. They were assigned to guard the beachheads and man the antiaircraft guns on the island. They assured us that the Japanese were well aware of their prowess and because of their presence, Corregidor was safe from any Japanese invasion.

Very soon after that welcome assurance, a formation of Japanese bombers escorted by Zero fighters appeared over Corregidor and for the first time, we were subjected to a withering air raid that lasted for half a day. For many of us, it was our first close-up exposure to earth-shattering bomb blasts, the roar of aircraft engines, and antiaircraft and machine gun fire. It was an unforgettable experience and it took a bit of the edge off of the assurances that the marines had just provided us.

The air raid occurred just as Colonel Wood and I were in the midst of translating a captured Japanese field order that MacArthur Headquarters was waiting for. During the raid, everything shook with the noise of the bombs exploding all around, causing the colonel and me to retreat into a shower stall in the Middleside barracks. Every time he heard the whistle of a falling bomb and its subsequent explosion, the colonel cussed. My comment to him was that my ancestors were meting out this punishment in angry retribution for translating the document. Colonel Wood never forgot that joking comment and I heard that he often repeated the incident to others when he was a prisoner of war.

On 26 December, just two days after my arrival in Corregidor, I was suddenly ordered to go to Bataan. The very mention of Bataan today immediately conjures up memories of the Death March and all the brutality and suffering associated with the place. But the Bataan that I first laid eyes on was simply beautiful. It was a place of virgin forests and verdant tropical growth. I remember vividly that when I got to the outdoor field mess, I felt like a Boy Scout at camp. The first thing that I had at the field mess was pancakes with syrup that tasted just heavenly. Another source of gustatory delight on Bataan before the fighting rudely intruded was the abundance of sarsaparilla in the forests. The existence of sarsaparilla was originally pointed out to the cooks by Col. Arthur F. Fisher. His knowledge of plants enabled us to have some great tasting root beer on Bataan. Unfortunately, almost overnight, fighting erupted on the Bataan Peninsula, bringing an end to the pleasant interlude. Thereafter, neither Bataan nor its beautiful forests would ever be the same.

When the fighting reached Bataan, I was either interrogating prisoners or trying to persuade the Japanese troops to surrender over the radio. Since we were unprepared to mount a comprehensive psychological warfare effort, the only other alternative open to us was to write surrender leaflets in Japanese, which we did as best as we could. Normally, the leaflets were air-dropped but by then, we had no air support.

However, once we ceded complete air superiority to the Japanese, we could no longer rely on airdrops. So we relied on some local field engineers to devise a crude slingshot device to hurl quarter-inch pipes cut into two-inch lengths stuffed with our propaganda leaflets behind enemy lines. The leaflets told the Japanese troops that they were being misled about the war by their ultramilitaristic leaders and that they were fighting a futile war since they would ultimately be overrun by American forces. They were told to "wise up" and return to the homeland where their loved ones awaited their return. We folded our leaflets and stuffed them into small pieces of pipe before popping them over into enemy lines. As amateurish as it may sound by today's standards, the prevailing rationale was that it was better than doing nothing.

Another method employed was the use of field amplifiers to talk to them. Whenever the amplifier was turned on, the Japanese would, for some reason, cease firing, to listen to what I was saying. As soon as I finished, they would start firing again, with even greater intensity.

I always wondered what sort of impact our psychological warfare was having on the enemy troops. Eventually, as I got to understand the Japanese better, I realized that the propaganda was having no effect at all. They were brought up to think differently from Americans and many of our enticements had no appeal to them. To the ordinary Japanese soldier, it was like black coffee not being his cup of green tea. What we were encountering at Bataan was a more seasoned breed of troops, many battle hardened in China and fanatically committed and patriotic.

This was borne out with prisoners that I interrogated who were stubborn beyond compare, refusing even to provide their real names. Many who were wounded or captured under circumstances beyond their control felt disgraced, preferring death to the shame of falling into enemy hands. Those falling within that category were incorrigible.

The fighting was furious by then and we were all thoroughly absorbed in holding off the attacks by fresh Japanese troops. As the battles raged, I was completely unaware that halfway around the world, Executive Order 9066 was just being issued, which led to the internment of some 110,000 ethnic Japanese on the West Coast of America. My experience on Bataan taught me that for mere mortals, there is no such thing as utter fearlessness in war. But in spite of fear and the horror and brutality of the fighting, Bataan was preferable to one of those internment camps. At least, no one questioned my loyalty to America on Bataan.

Although we continued to hope that help would somehow arrive from the United States, events around us were not encouraging. We were on the defensive against a tenacious foe and we were on half rations to preserve our food stocks for a long stand.

However, in early February, one engagement helped to cheer up our forces. One standard operating procedure observed by all units on patrol was to collect personal belongings from dead and wounded bodies for investigation by G2. During the latter part of January, a Filipino patrol working an area on the other side of Bataan discovered the body of a slain Japanese officer. They immediately collected everything from the body and sent it back to G2 for routine examination. In the course of examining the materials, I discovered a copy of an order that called for a key Japanese battalion to move up from the south to Quinauan Point. The responsibility of that battalion was to bolster units at key beachheads that had already been established on Luzon and join in mounting a major drive toward Mariveles.

This bit of intelligence enabled the American Command to position a tank battalion, troops, a few of the surviving P-40s and a few motor torpedo boats in key positions to surprise the Japanese flotilla transporting the battalion. In the ensuing battle, the enemy flotilla was badly mauled and repulsed. For those of us at Bataan, it was more than a tactical victory. It was a moral victory of considerable importance. It bolstered our will to fight on. The commander of the well-known Japanese battalion was killed during the aborted landing operation and his personal sword was forwarded to General MacArthur as a memento of our victorious stand against the seemingly unstoppable Japanese invasion force. To me, the discovery and translation of that key battle document was heartening and made all the long and frustrating hours of work worthwhile.

The one brief moment of euphoria was soon supplanted by the deterioration of conditions at Bataan. Nearly twenty-eight thousand men, the majority of them untrained, were involved in the withdrawal to Bataan in late December. Some units had to travel as much as 150 miles. By the time they arrived in Bataan, the force had dwindled to about sixteen thousand men. They were on the edge of exhaustion and barely had enough to eat during the retreat. The course of the fighting around Bataan was plotted on a huge map posted on one of the walls at headquarters and the indications were anything but good. Nevertheless, unlike our insular existance in Manila, we were now aware of how we were faring in the war on a day-to-day basis.

As time passed, it was disheartening to see the overall battle picture deteriorating in favor of the enemy. Every morning, as we surveyed the map, we could see that the U.S. forces were being pushed further south into the Bataan Peninsula. In January 1942, we were placed on reduced rations. According to reports, the evacuation of rations was not as successful as the evacuation of personnel into Bataan. Virtually every day, we got by on one meal of corned beef hash in the evening. Breakfast was a small serving of watered-down cereal and there was nothing for lunch.

On Bataan, I slept in a tent and on any given day, the searing tropical heat could be as unforgiving as the rainfall that soaked our tents, clothing, shoes, and blankets. As a kid on a camping trip I may have found such brushes with nature as something to laugh about in the comfort of a shady tree or around a raging campfire, but in our dire condition, all we could do was to wallow in extreme discomfort. We also did a lot of cursing, especially when hunger added to our sorry predicament.

Finally, in order to sustain us in the defense of Bataan for as long as possible, the Quartermaster Corps began slaughtering the cavalry horses to feed us. About once a week, we were given horse meat steaks and in our famished state, that was a feast! Whenever we received a shipment of the horse meat, our mess sergeant would make it a point to collect every scrap and bone from our allotment to make a special soup for lunch. On those rare occasions it did wonders to alleviate our hunger since we were usually not fed lunch.

In March 1942, I was ordered to leave Bataan for Corregidor. Although it was supposed to be temporary duty, I would not see Bataan again for a while. I departed for Corregidor on a small motorized launch. As we drew closer, the island fortress that I had left just a few months before seemed to rise out of the ocean.

The construction of fortifications on Corregidor began soon after the Philippines were ceded to the United States. At that time, it was aptly dubbed the "Gibraltar of the East." Aerial photos of the island show it to be shaped like a tadpole. The area at the head of the tadpole-shaped island was called Topside where the headquarters, barracks, officers' quarters, and parade grounds were located. The low area of the island was called Bottomside, where two docks, warehouses, a power plant, and cold storage were located. In the western section of the narrow piece of land that connected the head of the tadpole to the tail was Middleside. Directly east of Middleside was Malinta Hill where a maze of tunnels was built for defensive purposes. Beyond Malinta, where the island narrowed to form the tail of the tadpole, was a tiny airfield and a naval radio intercept station. Middleside was the location of the quarters that housed the commissioned and noncommissioned officers, the hospital, service club, and schools for the children of the island. A trolley car system linked the inhabitants to each of the main facilities. In all, Corregidor occupied no more than two miles of land, and it was about half a mile across at the widest point.

On Corregidor, I was assigned to work under Col. "Tiger" Teague, deciphering Japanese codes and monitoring Japanese radio frequencies. When enemy bombers took off from Clark Air Base on their bombing missions, there was voice communication between planes, which we monitored to determine where they were headed. Once we knew the target areas, we alerted the units around those areas so that they would be prepared for the air attacks. In that assignment, I worked very closely with Lieutenant Hoffcut and both of us normally worked between eighteen and twenty hours a day. The work was hard but operationally satisfying. We got results that paid off on the battlefield and that was more important than any-thing else. There was only one element of incongruity. People in the Signal Corps who prided themselves on the accuracy with which they transmitted and received information had trouble with my name, Sakakida. So they took their cue from Colonel Teague, who, aside from having trouble with my name, noted my hair-trigger temper and labeled me "Kelly." "Me, Irish?" I laughed. But the name stuck and that's how I was known to the guys in the Signal Corps.

While we did well in intercepting voice transmissions, it took a while for Hoffcut and me to get a grip on code deciphering. It took us about a month before we could forward deciphered intelligence to G2.

As the war worsened, Colonel Wood and Colonel Teague had become concerned about me. They were both very worried about my Japanese ancestry and about what would happen to me if we were to be overrun by the Japanese forces. Together, they decided that it would be best to get me off of Corregidor to continue my work at General MacArthur's headquarters in Australia.

There was normally a four-passenger aircraft that flew out of McKinley Field on Corregidor. It flew into an airstrip in Del Monte, Mindanao, where a B-17 picked up the passengers to be transported to Australia. All critical personnel were transported to Australia under those arrangements.

It was finally decided that I would be evacuated to Australia. Once that was determined, I packed a musette bag with minimal belongings so that I could leave on short notice at any time. One day, I was informed that I would be departing on a flight scheduled to leave at 11:00 P.M. I was elated beyond description. I was bone weary, hungry, and fearful of being captured by the Japanese.

Yet, strangely enough, in that brief moment of euphoria, I was visited by pangs of conscience. In war and in the fold of the U.S. Army, I had enjoyed a camaraderie with American troops and Filipino scouts that was as genuine and compelling as any collective relationship could be. It had nothing to do with race or ethnicity. It had everything to do with common cause and being collectively reduced by war to sharing intense loyalty, dedication, fear, hunger, privations, and insecurity on a real and elemental level. Somehow, living on the edge of survival day after day and hour after hour had thrust us onto a common level of human understanding. I couldn't walk away from such a condition without regard for the less fortunate. It was just at that moment that I thought about Clarence Yamagata, the former legal counsel for the Japanese Embassy in Manila who had gone out of his way to help me before the war broke out.

When the war came, he was imprisoned with the rest of the Japanese Embassy staff at Fort McKinley. As our Japanese-language resources became stretched beyond our limits at G2, I suggested that we get Clarence out of prison to assist us in our work. The G2 agreed and we raced into Manila to get him out of prison just as the Japanese invasion force was getting ready to enter the city. He was given no choice in the matter.

To this day, I do not know how he felt when he discovered my connection to army intelligence. He had every right to be upset at me for misleading him but he never ever displayed or voiced any animosity toward me. At that time, he personally showed every indication of understanding my situation. He was one of the most phlegmatic men that I had ever run into, never revealing any strong emotions to anyone except close acquaintances. He just accepted what we did to him and went right to work for us. He seemed like a nice guy and he was a hard worker.

I figured that under the circumstances, his capture by the Japanese would probably be fatal since he was a trusted member of the Japanese Embassy staff and he would immediately be suspected of being an enemy spy or turncoat. Moreover, his family had been evacuated to Japan and if they persisted in prosecuting him, his family would become a target for retribution. Also, he was a frail man who would probably not be able to take any harsh treatment in prison. During my stay on Bataan, I spent considerable time nursing him because of his many and varied ailments. I felt responsible for his predicament and I knew how I would feel if he were to face execution for what he did for us.

With that weighing on my conscience, I went to Colonel Wood with the proposal that Clarence leave Corregidor instead of me. He seemed stunned by my request.

"Why do you want to do that? Are you crazy?" he inquired.

"I was the happiest man on Corregidor when you told me I could leave," I replied. I cited all of my reasons, including what I regarded as a moral obligation that I had to fulfill.

The concept of *on*, or moral obligation, was too complex for me to explain to him. It is something that we owe to our Japanese forebears. I simply grew up steeped in the efficacy of the concept. It

91

involved a whole set of obligations that we learned to accept in relation to family, friends, community, and nation. It was also integral
to our identity. Because of what we were, we did accordingly. It
was a kind of moral force that cemented interpersonal relationships,
reinforced one's identity, and fostered community cohesiveness.
Looking after each other meant furthering the social betterment of
all of us. Thus, to profit at the expense of others was to err and to
give of oneself was necessary, no matter how painful. With my
mother, all of this was embodied in a fundamental rule by which
many of the Japanese-Americans lived: never bring shame to oneself,
one's family, or to our collective identity as Japanese-Americans.

Not everyone abided by those rules. All of this may sound improb-
able and overly idealistic but that's the way our generation was
raised in Hawaii. Unlike the others around me, Clarence treated me
like a Hawaiian. As a fellow Hawaiian and friend, I owed him at
least that much in return.

I didn't try to explain all of this to Colonel Wood. I simply emphasized that he was likely to be beheaded by the Japanese if he was
caught in the predicament that we had placed him in, that he had
a family that could suffer reprisals in Japan, that he was in very poor
health—also, he could carry on his work in Australia.

On the other hand, I told the colonel that I was single, I still had
a military obligation to meet, and that if we were to be overrun by
the enemy, I might be of some assistance to General Wainwright in
dealing with his Japanese counterparts. I didn't feel I was making a
heroic gesture; it just seemed like the decent thing to do under the
circumstances.

Colonel Wood conveyed my request to General Wainwright and
approval was granted in time to allow us to quickly transport Clarence out of the Philippines. Later, I was informed that General Wainwright was glad that I had volunteered to remain behind because he
needed me around if we had to surrender. In the brief interval before
takeoff, I provided Clarence with all of the information that I had
gathered on deciphering Japanese codes. I encouraged him to continue the operation in Australia.

Clarence's usual expressionless face lit up that night when he finally realized that he was being evacuated. He was a picture of joy

and relief and I was happy for him. Oddly, our paths never crossed again, even though we were stationed in Japan at the same time after the war. I understand that he received a field commission as a captain in Australia and returned to Japan as a major with General MacArthur's occupation staff after the surrender of Japan.

Bataan fell on 9 April 1942. With that, the Japanese high command turned its forces on Corregidor and we were thereafter subjected to incessant bombing and shelling. The air raid sorties joined by blistering artillery fire were continuous during the day. At night, there were no air raids, just the pounding of heavy artillery firing. Since I was situated deep down in the bowels of Malinta Tunnel, I was not in immediate danger from the bombing and shelling but I could see all around me that the stepped-up attacks were making us all nervous. All we could do was hope that help would arrive.

The code deciphering room where I worked branched off laterally from the Signal Corps tunnel and we occupied a space that took up one-third of the quartermaster tunnel. The only thing that separated us from the quartermaster storage was a hastily erected wall of boards nailed together.

By then, we were subsisting on very meager daily rations while working an average of twenty hours a day. One day, out of sheer hunger and an appetite for pranks that had somehow survived among all the suffering, we decided to make a special requisition courtesy of the Quartermaster Corps. Using all the stealth that we could muster, we loosened one of the boards from the partitioning to allow one man to squeeze into the adjoining storage area. The fellow who squeezed through to the other side picked up the first crate that he could lay his hands on and quickly passed it to us through the narrow crack in the wall. Had our risky breach of quartermaster requisition procedures been discovered, we would have faced stiff penalties under court-martial. So the whole operation was accomplished as fast as our weary bodies would allow us to move. As soon as we reboarded the crack in the retaining wall, we turned with rapt attention to the contents of the crate. A couple of the fellows pried the cover open and as they carefully removed the paper covering to the contents, we were all salivating. Our minds would only allow us to imagine a feast to fill our empty stomachs. When one of the fellows reached in and revealed the contents of of the crate, we were crushed by disappointment. The crate was full of shredded coconut, unsweetened and virtually tasteless. I cursed the quartermaster for requisitioning such food for the Philippines. What were they planning to do with it, make coconut cakes? We ended up adding the tasteless coconut shreds to our cereal every day to bulk it up for our breakfast. After a while, we were able to laugh about our rotten luck—maybe we had it coming for breaking regulations.

The stepped-up bombing and shelling every day clearly indicated that they were doing it with virtual impunity and that it was only a matter of time before an invasion of Corregidor would be attempted. The Japanese air raids, though incessant, did not have a crippling effect on our defenses. Neither did the long-range 105-mm howitzers. However, the shelling by captured British 240-mm guns used by the Japanese artillery units was devastating. The effect of the shelling on our beachhead defenses was to neutralize much of our artillery. According to General Wainwright, of the forty-eight 75-mm field guns positioned along the beaches, forty-six were knocked out of commission before the enemy landings began.

One day, I was called by Colonel Wood. He looked tired and drawn when I entered his office, but he made every effort to appear undaunted by the circumstances. After a casual exchange of greetings, he sat down and asked seriously, "Do you have any gut feeling about when they plan to land their troops on Corregidor?"

I thought about it for a while and replied, "The way things are, they could attempt a landing at any time, but if we are to look for omens, there are two dates that stand out."

"What are those dates and why are they important?" he inquired with obvious interest.

"Well," I replied with some hesitation, "April 28 is the emperor's birthday and May 5 is Boy's Day, an important holiday in Japan." The importance of the emperor's birthday speaks for itself. On the other hand, Boy's Day has been celebrated in Japan for centuries and it has traditionally stressed the importance of honor, manhood, bravery, and strength as desired attributes of all boys growing up in Japan. Decorative horses were prominently displayed on those occasions to symbolize those virtues and so were paper-balloon carp hoisted atop poles into the wind, making them look like real fish swimming in the air. The carp is also an important symbol because of its ability to fight its way up streams and because of its determination to overcome obstacles. I added, "That doesn't necessarily mean that they have to attack on those days but they have been known to take advantage of auspicious days to plan their attacks or to heighten the significance of some of their battlefield initiatives. Right now, those two dates come to mind. My own feeling is that April 29 is the primary date and May 5 the secondary date."

"Very interesting," he said. "I'll keep that in mind." We talked a little more and I left to go back to the Signal Corps lateral.

There was no invasion on 29 April but the bombing and shelling on that day was particularly intense. My primary hunch did not pan out. However, around midnight on the night of 4 May, a message came in that a large force of Japanese landing barges had been sighted heading toward Corregidor. By 5 May, the Japanese had landed troops simultaneously at Corregidor, Fort Hughes, Fort Drum, and Cabrillo Island, thereby neutralizing the four U.S. fortresses guarding the approaches to Manila Bay.

Although our men fought gallantly to inflict heavy casualties on the enemy invaders, in the end, we were overrun by them. The size of the Japanese invasion force was overwhelming, and by then, everyone on our side had reached the limits of hunger and exhaustion. For all of us holding out on the rock, we had finally reached the depth of despair.

For months and against all odds, I had suppressed all thoughts about the possibility of our surrender. But when the defenses of Corregidor were breached, it was time to think about what was until then, unthinkable. In reality, death would have been an easier alternative for me. Yet, duty kept beckoning. I kept reminding myself of Major Raymond's orders to stick with my original mission. My only hope of carrying out the mission was to stick to my cover story, as unlikely as that hope was with the imminence of the total Japanese takeover. Besides, I was supposed to be available to aid General Wainwright with his negotiations on the final terms of surrender. Fate had dealt me a lousy hand, and I had no choice but to play those cards.

The Sakakida family in 1928. Richard is at the far left.

Richard Sakakida in 1939
as he graduated from
high school.

Sakakida (right) en route to the Philippines on board the USAT *Republic* in April 1941 with Arthur Komori (left) and O'Neill.

General Homma, leader of the Japanese forces in the Philippines, inspects the battle-field after the invasion force landing. (*Courtesy of the National Archives*)

After the fall of Bataan, American soldiers were brutally treated on the Bataan Death March. (*Courtesy of the National Archives*)

Lieutenant General
Jonathan Wainwright
broadcasting the
announcement of the
surrender of Corregidor
in the Philippines.
(*Courtesy of the
National Archives*)

A U.S. surrender party being escorted by the Japanese in the Philippines.
(*Courtesy of the National Archives*)

Surrender negotiations between General Wainwright and Lieutenant General Homma.
(*Courtesy of the National Archives*)

American forces surrendering at Corregidor. (*Courtesy of the National Archives*)

Japanese tanks entering Manila. (*Courtesy of the National Archives*)

U.S. soldiers enter Manila after the Japanese surrender at the end of the war. Note the destruction of the city. (*Courtesy of the National Archives*)

Member of the Igorot tribe who helped Richard Sakakida recover after escaping from the Japanese at Baguio. (*Courtesy of the National Archives*)

Filipino guerrillas who operated behind the lines during Japanese occupation, many of whom escaped during a jailbreak staged by Richard Sakakida.
(*Courtesy of the National Archives*)

Sakakida in Manila in 1946, after the end of World War II.
(*Courtesy of the National Archives*)

Sakakida upon retirement from the Air Force in April 1975.

Ambassador Paul Rabe presents Richard Sakakida with the Philippine Legion of Honor Award at the Philippine Embassy in Washington, D.C., April 15, 1994. Sakakida's wife is on the right.

Chapter 7

SURRENDER AT CORREGIDOR

The surrender of Corregidor on 6 May 1942 was a bitter pill to swallow. That event was preceded on 24 April by the arrival of the last of the prisoners in the Bataan Death March at Camp O'Donnell, thus ending one of the most brutal episodes of the Philippine campaign. Their arrival occurred just twelve days prior to the surrender of Corregidor. By then, the downfall of Corregidor may have been inevitable but many of us denied the inevitable until the bitter end.

But even in surrender, there was some consolation. First of all, we still had hope—it was not the end yet. In addition, the victory was no walkover for the Japanese. The plan drawn up at Japanese Imperial Headquarters prior to the war called for the conquest of Luzon by January. We had upset that timetable by four months and given the United States some time to recover from the shock of the initial setbacks in the Pacific.

The toll of American and Filipino casualties was high and therefore tragic. But the casualties inflicted on the Japanese side were also high. For example, according to a history compiled by an organization of the Defenders of Bataan and Corregidor, at Bataan, the Japanese 65th Brigade started out with 6,651 officers and men on 9 January. By 24 January, the brigade had suffered 1,972 casualties, most of them inflicted on its three infantry regiments. From 6 January 1942 to 1 March 1942, the Japanese 14th Army suffered about 7,000 casualties: approximately 2,700 dead and over 4,000 wounded. Another ten to twelve thousand men were stricken with malaria, beriberi, dysentery, and other tropical diseases, which reduced its rolls to almost nothing.

On the American side, one unraveling feature of the Philippine campaign was the lack of adequate rations. While the lack of food was but one of a number of glaring deficiencies that contributed to the downfall of the Philippines, it undoubtedly hastened the surrender. The situation was exacerbated by the arrival of thousands of civilians from places such as Manila who came on their own in advance of the Japanese forces. They, too, had to be fed from the dwindling stock of military rations. During the exodus to Bataan, the level of food supplies transported did not even begin to match the number of people arriving there.

Prior to the outbreak of war, the caloric intake per man was set at about 5,000 calories a day. On 6 January 1942, the level was reduced to 3,000 calories a day. On 1 February 1942, the level was cut to less than 1,500 a day. On 1 March 1942, it was cut further to 1,000 calories a day. Many of us were reduced to eating wild animals. On Bataan, we ate rattlesnakes, monkeys, and iguana. I put monkeys at the bottom of the list of things I ate to avert starvation. Their resemblance to humans was much too close for me. It is a wonder that so many of our men held out for so long with uncommon valor and endurance. For the men who were forced into the Bataan Death March after the cease-fire, their emaciated condition only compounded the "journey into hell." By the time I left Bataan, I too had contracted malaria, beriberi, and dysentery. It could have been worse. Had I not been abruptly transferred to Corregidor, I could very well have been part of that infamous march too.

In war there is nothing worse than losing. There was nothing to be ashamed of in the way we went down first in Bataan and then in Corregidor, but in the wake of surrender, I felt myself being pulled

into a spiral of gloom where I had all I could handle to hold on to
my self-esteem.

The early success achieved by the Japanese military in Asia and
the Pacific was phenomenal. In the Philippines, they came prepared
for an all-out offensive. We were not prepared for that. All we could
do was to buy some time. We were outdone not just in number but
also in training and experience, we were outgunned with superior
technology, and in many cases, we were outfoxed. At this stage of
the war, the Japanese Zero fighter plane, their use of auxiliary fuel
tanks to provide fighter cover for their bombers, their mechanized
equipment, and modern communications systems were much better
than what we had at our disposal. Once the fighting started in the
Philippines, the odds virtually assured a Japanese victory.

By delaying what seemed assured, we diminished their reputation
for invincibility. It allowed the galvanization of a national will and
the mobilization of our vast industrial and manpower resources.

We were unaware that there were changes already underway. The
surprise Doolittle raid on Tokyo on 18 April, followed by critical
victories that were soon to follow in the Battle of Coral Sea on 7–8
May and the Battle of Midway on 3–6 June, would begin the slow
process of turning things around in our favor.

But we were in Corregidor and only knew that surrender was set
for noon on 6 May 1942 by General Wainwright. At 10:15 A.M., he
ordered General Beebe to arrange for the broadcast of a surrender
message. It was to be a joint effort involving General Beebe and
myself. At exactly 10:30 A.M., the general stepped to the microphone
at the radio station on Corregidor dubbed the "Voice of Freedom"
by General MacArthur and broadcast the call, "Message for General
Homma, message for General Homma." He then broadcast the surrender message in English. I immediately followed General Beebe,
broadcasting the same message in Japanese.

Essentially, the message stated that at twelve noon a white flag
would be raised on Corregidor, at which time all firing would cease
on the U.S. side. Once the firing stopped, General Wainwright would
send two members of his staff on a boat carrying a white flag to
Cabcaben dock to meet with a staff officer representing General
Homma to arrange for the formal surrender and other details. Upon

the return of his own staff officers, General Wainwright would take his staff to meet with General Homma at a site to be determined by the Japanese.

The surrender was complicated by a number of prior restrictions placed on General Wainwright. One particularly sticky point was that before his departure from the Philippines for Australia, General MacArthur created four separate commands for the continuing defense of the Philippines. All four commands in the Philippines were to remain under his command in Australia. The idea was to prevent a complete collapse of the defense of the Philippines in the event that Bataan and Corregidor should be overrun by the Japanese. Should this happen, he had hoped that remnants of the U.S. forces would join up with the Philippine scouts to form a guerrilla force in the islands.

Because of that stipulation, in his first meeting with the Japanese side, which General Wainwright was forced to attend because the Japanese refused to talk to any of his staff officers, he felt free to offer up only the four fortified islands guarding the approaches to Manila Bay.

The English-speaking junior officer representing the Japanese loudly responded that General Homma could accept nothing less than the surrender of all American and Philippine troops from the designated commander of all U.S. forces in the Philippines.

General Wainwright wisely deflected the insolent demand of the young officer by insisting that such a decision would have to be deferred until he was allowed to meet personally with General Homma. At that point, a Japanese colonel interceded, agreeing to take Wainwright and his staff to Cabcaben in Bataan to meet with Homma under the terms of the surrender statement broadcast that morning. General Wainwright then returned to Corregidor to form a team to accompany him to the next meeting.

General Wainwright quickly collected his staff to meet with General Homma, and General Beebe told me that I would be a member of the group. I dressed in a khaki uniform completely bereft of military markings and insignias to protect my cover story that I was a civilian employee.

As we departed by boat from Corregidor, a Japanese fighter plane hovered over us, monitoring our every move as we headed toward Cabcaben. When we got to the docking area, we were ordered to line up in a single file and identify ourselves. This was demanded of each of us by a Japanese sergeant major.

Apparently, the Japanese POWs that I had interrogated in Manila had identified me as the Japanese-American doing all the broadcasting on the American side. When we retreated to Bataan, we had left the POWs behind. When he got to me, the sergeant major looked at me with utter contempt and asked, "Are you a Filipino?"

Without hesitation, I replied, "No sir, I am an American."

Apparently, he didn't like that coming from a nonwhite. But whatever the reason, he suddenly punched me in the face, shattering my glasses. It happened so fast that he caught me completely by surprise. The first thing I realized was that the force of the blow had knocked me down and blood was streaming down my face from cuts inflicted by the glass shards from my shattered eyeglasses. He had hit me in the eye and he could easily have blinded me. The taste of blood is unforgettable whether inflicted in war, sports, or a fist fight. Oddly enough, in tense confrontations it can have a steadying effect. The blow quickly purged me of whatever fear or worry I had harbored during that short boat ride over from Corregidor. I felt like punching him back. I had always been known for my quick temper when provoked and what the sergeant did to me was an extreme provocation, in my book.

Needless to say, I was livid with rage. Actually, it was nothing compared to a street brawl in Palama and pain had nothing to do with the real source of my rage. What really got to me was the utter contempt with which he humiliated me in front of everyone at the dock. The one thing I remember well was General Beebe, who was aware of my temper, shouting, "Hold your temper, Kelly." I realized that it was too important an event for me to disrupt so I bit my lip and remained mute. But I vowed then and there that I would die rather than give my Japanese captors any kind of confession or forced statement.

It was a sobering experience that was full of symbolism. When the sergeant major broke my glasses, he broke the proverbial "rose-colored glasses" through which I had been taught in Hawaii to view all things Japanese. With a single blow, my illusions were shattered. So much for the Japanese community propaganda that I had learned to respect as a kid. As for my glasses, they were never replaced and I would go through all the years as a POW unable to see clearly. Perhaps it was just as well.

Growing up in Hawaii, I may have been considered a minority by some people but it was something that I hardly ever even thought about—in reality, the Japanese constituted the largest ethnic group in the islands. Moreover, one of the overriding advantages of growing up in the Hawaii of old was the presence of a polyglot society that gave free reign to the expression of various ethnic cultures. Even today, it is the one place that I know of in this world where ethnic jokes play such a prominent role as a source of shared comic relief rather than as a source of serious misunderstanding. I learned very quickly that "thinking local, acting universal," was a naive assumption in time of war. To people like the sergeant major, I was not worthy of respect as a Japanese or an American. One thing was for sure—the incident was the first blatant act of discrimination that I had ever experienced in my life and the irony of it all was that it came from an ethnic Japanese soldier. It made me an even more committed American. He could deprive me of my freedom, but he could not deprive me of my identity.

After he hit me, the sergeant major ordered three soldiers standing by to take me to another part of the dock to watch me. He then told me that I was not needed by General Wainwright and his staff; that the Japanese side would provide its own interpreters. I could see helplessness on the faces of the Americans and there were protests, but to no avail. I tried as hard as I could to muster a smile and told them to go ahead without me. So I was left at the dock while the rest of the American group proceeded to Cabcaben. General Beebe, obviously moved by the incident, told me to hold on and I told him not to worry.

The soldiers left to watch over me were an uneasy lot, disconcerted by what had happened. As soldiers, they were used to brutal treatment from their officers and noncoms and they betrayed signs of sympathy for me but they had to cover it up. They would occasionally glance at me, their prisoner, who looked something like them but was obviously not one of them.

Later that evening General Wainwright's team came back to the dock and I was allowed to accompany them back to Corregidor. We were escorted back by a young Japanese lieutenant who was also identified as an intelligence officer who was fluent in English. Because of that, General Wainwright and his staff maintained complete silence throughout the return trip.

I don't know whether the lieutenant was aware of what had happened at the dock, but he approached me and struck up a conversation. He tried to be very sympathetic and he informed me that the Japanese people who were detained at the Nippon Club were quite concerned about what had happened to me after I was dragged out unceremoniously from the club premises. He told me they were all concerned about my health and wondered how the Americans were treating me. He obviously wanted information from me, and he asked whether I had been paid by the U.S. Army. I said I was given food and a place to sleep and that being paid was of secondary concern to me since there was no way I could spend it anyway.

I knew at this point that it was crucial to preserve my cover. Surrender was upon us. I knew the lieutenant's sympathy was a ploy, and I had to be careful not to compromise myself with any loose talk.

Colonel Pugh, who had succeeded Colonel Wood as G2, had informed me that I would be listed as a civilian on the surrender list. My Japanese ancestry and my work in intelligence would have been a sure formula for a Japanese death penalty.

The colonel added that if I survived the interrogation process and succeeded in holding to my cover story, I should still carry on my basic mission by working myself into positions that would allow me to carry on my mission in espionage. As a special agent I had no problem with that request.

Upon our return to Corregidor, we learned that General Wainwright had been unable to prevail in setting the terms of surrender. The Japanese high command knew that when MacArthur departed the Philippines for Australia, he had turned over the command of U.S. forces to Wainwright. His proposal to give up just the four fortresses was unacceptable. In the end, General Homma left him no real alternative. Homma threatened to complete the invasion of Corregidor and annihilate everyone there if General Wainwright insisted on a partial surrender. The invading Japanese forces were already near some of the key tunnel entrances and had they been allowed to bring their tanks and big guns up to the tunnel entrances, there would have been a level of slaughter too cruel to even contemplate. To prevent what would certainly have resulted in a massacre, Wainwright agreed to Homma's surrender terms. General Wainwright was later criticized for this decision, but in the minds of every one of his staff officers who were there with him to the very end, his decision was justified.

Preparations for the surrender, which was scheduled to take place the next day, 7 May 1942, began at once. There were things that we did not want to fall into enemy hands. I immediately set about destroying all of my code-deciphering materials and files. I also helped dispose of a huge cache of unissued U.S. currency that was stored at Malinta Tunnel. All remaining greenbacks had to be cut into pieces. Conditions in the tunnel prevented us from burning them. It was hot and stuffy in the tunnel and my face still smarted as the salt from my own perspiration dripped into the cuts that I suffered earlier that day. But we worked quickly, focusing only on the task at hand.

Later, I went over my belongings. I had to be sure that nothing in my possession reflected any connection with the U.S. Army. I rechecked my khaki uniform for any telltale signs, and once I was convinced that it was clean of any markings, I laid it aside.

The sound of occasional gunfire and sporadic fighting resonated through the tunnel and casualties continued to be brought in throughout the night. When the sun rose on the morning of 7 May 1942, time had finally run out on us.

Our sleeping quarters at Malinta Tunnel consisted of rows of three-tiered bunks. I lay in my bunk, staring at the dark walls and curved ceiling. The inner shell was formidable, made with eighteen inches of reinforced concrete, which had kept us safe from gunfire but not from Japanese ground forces that would soon be marching in to occupy our quarters. As I gazed at the lines of the rafters arching upward in support of the massively thick ceiling, a thought suddenly occurred to me. The only thing of value that I had was the Elgin watch my mother had given me at graduation. I was not about to let that fall in enemy hands. I quickly climbed onto a ledge bordering the rafter above me to look for an obscure cranny where I could conceal it. Luckily, there was a place so I unstrapped my watch and placed it there.

Later on, after we were searched and all of our personal effects had been confiscated, and after I learned that I would be kept in Corregidor for a while, I snuck back to retrieve my watch. Over the next year my watch would tell me more than time—it would figure in some surprising incidents.

We had done all we could to destroy everything of potential use to the enemy but that, of course, was impossible. As I lay on my bunk, I hoped I had destroyed everything that could ruin my cover story. I was weary beyond description, but even that could not stay the numbing realization that I would soon be in Japanese hands and there was no telling what was in store for me. Anger, uncertainty, sadness, fear, despair, and a whole host of other conflicting emotions simultaneously welled up inside of me. All around me lay a troubled silence that said I was not alone in trying to maintain control. It was like sitting in a locker room after a particularly bruising and disheartening loss. This time, the stakes were much higher and there was no one around to cheer us up.

American GIs have always had a gift of making light of difficult circumstances, but on that day, the good-natured joshing and bantering were gone. There was very little said. Finally, the spell of dour contemplation was broken when we were ordered to report to the entrance of Malinta Tunnel and get into formation for the surrender.

Along with General Wainwright and his staff, we lined up on both sides of Malinta Tunnel to await the entry of the Japanese forces. I had the pleasure of standing right by the general. The day of the surrender was the saddest day of my long military career. Neither the euphoria of the victorious end to World War II nor the happiness that I have had the good fortune to enjoy since retirement will ever erase the poignant sadness that I experienced that day on Corregidor. I shall never forget the sight of General Wainwright, dignified and unbowed, moving forward, while we stood at attention, to un-buckle his belt and holster with pearl-handled pistol in symbolic recognition of the surrender. I could feel tears welling up in my eyes and I was sure that I was not alone in paying silent tribute to our commander who was there with us to the very end.

Soon after we were assembled, the 37th Japanese Infantry Battalion marched into Malinta Tunnel with fixed bayonets and full combat gear to accept the final surrender of Corregidor. It was a sight to behold. They came marching in perfect order, high stepping, arms swinging smartly in unison. Every time the metal rivets on the soles of their combat boots hit the concrete pavement, they made a fearsome sound that reverberated through the tunnel. The tattoo that they sounded in cadence with every step created a powerful and mesmerizing drumbeat that generated a crescendo of ominous sounds as they marched even deeper into the tunnel.

All of the soldiers wore cotton flaps that draped from their service caps like the headgear of the French Foreign Legion. In the dim recesses of the tunnel, the visual effect created by the flaps was eerie, dark, and forbidding. Like a troop of Darth Vaders they appeared sinister and menacing. They all carried rifles inscribed with the sixteen-petal imperial seal. It was said that woe be onto any soldier caught handling such rifles without proper care or respect.

The sights and sounds of that event are still in my mind, brilliant and deafening, over half a century after they occurred—so intense was that experience. What we saw that day seemed calculated to rebut the prevailing Western stereotype of Asia and Asians. They were seen as militarily weak and culturally backward, as purveyors of cheap trinkets and shoddy products. Treated as less than equals, they developed an upstart image steeped in cartoon caricaturizations highlighting their most unflattering features. Although the lesson was painful, the United States was being taught that Japan was different—modern, militaristic, and aggressive. It was a force to be reckoned with, not belittled.

Immediately after the brief ceremony, General Wainwright and his staff officers were escorted away. Although he was kind enough to write to me after the war, that was the last time that I would lay eyes on him.

From then on, there was nothing to do but to await the dreaded orders of our captors. After the incident on the way to Cabcaben, I was prepared for the worst. I experienced the terrible sensation of being trapped for the first time in my life.

I thought about my family and particularly my mother back in Hawaii. Before the surrender, I had been far too preoccupied with my duties and responsibilities to correspond much with my family, but at least I could have. Now, I would not be able to contact them and I could imagine their thoughts as they heard news of the downfall of the Philippines. Fortunately, although I was not aware of it at that time, Colonel Gilbert, who recruited me in Hawaii, visited my mother to try to cheer her up. It would have been reassuring to have known that as I stood in line in Malinta Tunnel awaiting what I thought might be my final fate. As brief as the waiting was, it was agonizing. At least I had gotten control of my thoughts and I was determined not to crack under any kind of pressure or torture.

We stood at attention to the very end, in single file and with our backs to the wall. As soon as the order was given, the general and his staff stepped out in formation and marched past the troops for the last time. I had no idea what would happen to me after their departure.

Chapter 8

FIRST BRUSH WITH IMPRISONMENT

Following the call-out of Wainwright and his staff, my name was called. I experienced a chilling sensation and tried as hard as I could to collect my wits as I was escorted to the office of the commander of the military "thought police," better known as the dreaded Kempeitai (*kempei* literally means military police and *tai* is a unit designator).

The Kempeitai had a reputation for terror and intimidation that virtually destroyed political liberalism and freedom in Japan in the 1930s and paved the way for the rise of Japanese militarism. Members could be identified by the white armbands they wore with red characters *Kempei* printed on them. When I realized where I was headed, I braced myself for the worst.

When we were growing up, many of the *isseis* could not read English so they taught us by reading us Japanese fables and fairy tales. They spent hours reading to us and also explaining what those lessons were supposed to mean to our lives. Storybooks and fables were a significant part of our Japanese-language school education.

117

Much of the stories were grounded in mythology but the stories seemed real to us because of the earnestness with which they were presented. My parents wanted those stories to serve as foundations for character and manhood. Early on, I loved the world of the samurai. As I faced becoming a POW, I wanted to live up the the highest ideals of a samurai. I had to accept fate on those terms and refrain from blaming others for my fate lest I end up wallowing in remorse, self-pity, and bitter hatred. It was the only way I could think of to avoid caving in to my captors.

The first encounter began innocently enough. The commander occupied a hastily set up office in the Malinta Tunnel complex. The first thing I saw as I entered was a huge stockpile of canned goods and cartons of American cigarettes confiscated from our quartermaster warehouse.

I reported to him looking haggard, bedraggled, and emaciated. He must have noticed how I gazed in surprise at the pile of food. He looked me over very quickly, then pointed to the food and to my surprise, asked me, "What is your wish?" I could hardly believe what he said to me. I didn't even stop to wonder whether he was acting out of compassion or just setting me up with hunger gnawing at my innards. I was not about to quibble over something as complex as intent. "If possible, I would like something sweet," I replied without hesitation.

He reached out, pulled out a can of Eagle Brand Condensed Milk and had one of his orderlies open it. He took it from the orderly, handed it to me and told me to go out of the tunnel to eat it before returning for the interrogation.

I have never been even remotely connected with the drug scene but looking back, I can imagine myself resembling a junkie in dire need miraculously happening on a fix. I greedily slurped, sucked, and licked every bit of the sticky contents and all the while, I remained completely oblivious to anything or anyone around me. It didn't matter who was watching, I devoured the entire can of condensed milk in no time at all. It tasted wonderful. It ended all too soon but it allowed me to collect my thoughts before going back into the tunnel to face my interrogators.

I had one grave concern at the outset. It had to do with an over-

118

sight by Captain Beebe, the custodian of my permanent file in Manila, who forgot to destroy it during the hurried exodus from the city in December 1941. When he got to Bataan, he realized that my service record, identifying photograph, and promotion orders were all left behind in the safe. I lived with the nightmare that upon entering Manila, the Japanese occupation personnel had gone through everything with a fine-tooth comb, especially the records that remained in the office formerly occupied by U.S. Army intelligence. I didn't know whether they had discovered those records. I prayed that they had not. Nevertheless, I intended to stick to my cover story.

The initial interrogation lasted two days and I became quite adept at telling my story. I told them that the U.S. Army was suffering from a serious shortage of Japanese linguists, which necessitated hiring me in desperation as a civilian employee. I emphasized the predicament that I faced as a civilian employee working for the army, a situation the army justified to me as an obligation that I owed the nation as an American citizen. I said I had no special skills and that when I interrogated, I merely followed a checklist of questions provided me by the army. Furthermore, I stated that in monitoring Japanese voice traffic over the airways, my effectiveness was limited because of my poor grasp of military science, tactics, and terminology.

The colonel then questioned me about my citizenship. Prior to World War II, it was common practice for immigrant parents to register the birth of their children at the Japanese Consulate in Honolulu. Some did it out of a sense of insecurity. As immigrant contract laborers, they were aware that they had little recourse to due process as we know it today and they were stateless. Others did it because they were told to do so. Moreover, when they first left Japan for Hawaii, the thought of war breaking out between the United States and Japan was the farthest thing from their minds. Regardless, I added, it was not something that was thoroughly considered by these parents, most of whom were poorly educated and were struggling to survive when they first came to the islands. The upshot of the matter was that many of the children became dual citizens without even being aware of it themselves. Many parents never even mentioned it to their children and some simply forgot about it.

Once the registrations were received at the consulate, they were sent to Japan to be documented in family registers maintained there. It then became a matter of permanent record. I was aware that my mother had filed expatriation papers with the Japanese Consulate in Honolulu after I joined the army so I was safe. However, I feigned ignorance and told him that since many first-generation parents had registered their children with the Japanese government, I assumed that I was in the same category. Lulled into complacency by my mother's wise decision to revoke my Japanese citizenship, I had not stopped to really consider the full implication of my citizenship status had the charge of treason been leveled against me. Fortunately, it was a mental lapse that I did not have to pay for.

The colonel was ever so adroit in his reply to my explanation. He stated that regardless of my citizenship, since I was born of Japanese parents, he considered me a full-blooded Japanese and, speaking as one Japanese to another, he felt compelled to ask me whether I felt it was a disgrace to be caught in the predicament that I found myself in. He asked me whether I had considered suicide as an alternative to being captured.

I replied that I had in fact considered suicide but that I had been deterred by the fact that I had left home despite my mother's objections and since she was unaware of my whereabouts, I was honor-bound to survive to somehow repay her for all the anguish and hardship that I had caused her. Committing suicide, I said to him, would only have compounded her grief. Besides, it would have been an easy way out for me. My rationale may have sounded corny to American ears, but it struck a responsive chord with the colonel who then launched into a lengthy lecture on the importance of loyalty and filial piety. He at least made the gesture of conveying some sympathy to me for all that I had to endure.

He also found it significant enough to inform me that the Japanese at the Nippon Club were greatly concerned about my welfare. They felt that it was their request for help in procuring food and other items that had gotten me into trouble with the American and Philippine authorities.

The colonel was obviously tough and well informed. Although he did not drive me to the edge, he really didn't have to. He had others

120

under him to do the job. He ended by informing me that I would temporarily be turned over to a major in command of the garrison at Corregidor.

Soon after being dismissed from the colonel's office, I was assigned to the 92d Garage Area where all of the U.S. and Philippine POWs were temporarily confined. Our former living quarters were immediately occupied by the Japanese troops, so we slept on the floor of a huge warehouse. At night, when we slept, it was wall-to-wall bodies. Worst of all, summer had come to the Philippines and the sweltering heat at night made sound sleep well-nigh impossible.

It was during my assignment to the 92d that I became acquainted with Father Albert Braun, a major in the U.S. Army Corps of Chaplains. Father Braun was intent on collecting and identifying the remains of Americans who were killed in action, but he found himself stymied by his inability to communicate with the Japanese officer in command of the prison camp. When he heard about me, he sought me out for assistance. He struck me as a man of obvious compassion and dedication so I was happy to escort him to a captain's office to communicate his wishes.

The captain was quite receptive to the chaplain's request since the Japanese themselves were eager to get on with the task of cleaning up the battered fort and consolidating their operations on the island. Father Braun was given blanket approval and was granted written permission to go about the task of recovering the remains of our fallen soldiers.

Two weeks following the surrender, three Japanese transport ships arrived in Corregidor to move all American and Filipino POWs to Manila. The Filipino POWs were placed on two of the ships and the Americans occupied the other.

When I first heard of the arrangement, I was mystified. After all, there were more American than Filipino soldiers. And yet, there were two ships for the Filipinos and one for the Americans. I finally realized that we were into mind games. The Filipinos had all the room in the world on the two ships while the Americans were herded together like cattle. It was virtually standing room only for the American POWs.

I was placed on board one of the Filipino ships, both of which

121

docked at the pier in Manila proper. I doubt whether they put me on that ship because I looked Asian. I think they wanted me along to serve as an interpreter for the Japanese crew when they got to the pier in Manila.

Just before we got to Manila, the drama unfolded. The ship carrying the American POWs did not sail into Manila Harbor. Instead, they moved the ship as close as possible to shore and anchored at a point near the south end of Dewey Boulevard. The Americans were ordered to jump into the water and wade ashore. For most of them, the water was up to their chests or even higher. It was a struggle to get ashore and some of our soldiers barely made it. Once on shore, the men were assembled and marched in columns of four down Dewey Boulevard, on to Quezon Boulevard, and finally to the old Bilibid Prison.

It was again a show of force, but this time it was for Filipino eyes. By marching the American captives through the streets of Manila, they hoped to impress the Filipinos with the prowess of the Japanese Army. At that time, I was not aware of the significance of the two-week interval between the surrender and the evacuation of prisoners from Corregidor. I learned later that the purpose was to hold the American and Filipino prisoners on Corregidor as hostages until the final surrender of all American and Filipino forces in the southern islands of the Philippines.

On board the ship that I took from Corregidor to Manila, some of the Japanese soldiers from the garrison at Corregidor who were performing escort duty systematically gathered about ten to fifteen Filipino soldiers at a time and confiscated their money and valuables. I watched with disgust what was occurring. I looked around but there were no officers on board. In hindsight, I think they purposely excluded them and used me to tell the the Filipinos what to do. Given the circumstances, the officers would probably not have allowed such a thing to happen. Of course, I may have been wrong but once, after the surrender, when I complained to an officer about a Japanese soldier laying down on an American flag as a breech of honor, he quickly reprimanded the soldier and had him turn the flag in. I learned later that the lieutenant was a reserve officer who had been called to active duty from the business world and that he still had a higher regard for honor and propriety than some of his more hard-bitten fellow officers.

But there was only one senior noncommissioned officer on board our ship, who not only seemed oblivious to the goings-on, he seemed to be behind it all. The soldiers used the money confiscated to enjoy themselves during their overnight stay in Manila.

When we got to Manila, I was informed by the noncommissioned officer in charge, a sergeant major, that I would for some reason be returning to Corregidor next morning. Meanwhile, I was confined to the ship for the night with some of the guards. It was a night for solitary contemplation for me as none of the guards said a word to me. They were probably upset at not being in downtown Manila and instead being on board ship with a POW. Early next morning, we departed for Corregidor. The sergeant major and those who went ashore the night before seemed none the worse for the wear after a rollicking night on the town. I missed Manila but it was just as well that I did not see the city on their terms. I felt more comfortable with old memories of the city.

My primary duty at Corregidor was to serve as the dispatcher for the motor pool, which was operationally entrusted to sixteen American POWs. The only American POWs left on Corregidor were members of the Engineer Corps commanded by Major John Dean Woodroth. Their responsibility was to restore to operation and thereafter maintain the American-made equipment and facilities on Corregidor.

For the next ninety days I worked as a dispatcher, arranging transportation for garrison headquarters. A Japanese sergeant and a so-called superior private were assigned to supervise the motor pool group. It was a loose organizational arrangement that practically allowed us to run the place on our own terms.

During the restoration of operations and facilities at Corregidor and at all of the rest of the major installations on Luzon, the Japanese were too busy to be preoccupied with us. The hiatus provided some of us with a welcome respite from months of fighting and unremitting duress, and we needed no coaxing to make the best of a situation that was likely to be temporary. For a brief period, our unit on Corregidor was blessed with good fortune.

123

Our first good luck was the assignment to our unit of marine sergeant Nolan, who had been running the marine mess. Since we were allowed to run our own mess, he was the logical choice to handle our mess needs. Like the fabled mess sergeants of old, he was full of army-style guile and resourcefulness. Even with the prospect of surrender staring him in the face, he had the presence of mind to stash away precious stores of flour, sugar, and various other staples in obscure nooks and crannies of the tunnel. It was a tribute to him that his cache evaded the prying eyes of even the most determined Japanese occupants of Malinta Tunnel. But then, Malinta was a huge complex. With the permission of the Japanese sergeant in charge of the motor pool, who was unaware of our plans, we took a five-ton truck to the tunnel to reclaim our treasure trove of food. It was an incredible windfall for us. For that reason, we were able to enjoy freshly baked bread every three days instead of staying with the regular supply of rice delivered to us by the Japanese garrison.

Once a week, the Japanese Quartermaster Corps sent over a boat-load of provisions to the Corregidor garrison from Manila. Whenever the boats arrived, we were ordered to provide the transportation and the labor required to unload the provisions at dockside and deliver them to the Japanese mess hall. On those occasions, we were fortunate to have a marine named Monahan along with us. If Sergeant Nolan was our source of gastronomical delights, it was Monahan who provided us with humor. Good food and good humor allowed us to maintain our composure and our sense of perspective and we owed it all to one source—the United States Marines.

Monahan regaled us with jokes to lighten every task and he never let an opportunity pass without the benefit of some searing comment. He was also a genius at setting up people and events as foils for his brand of humor. He was a rough-hewn wiseacre, a cutup, and he had refined street smarts. Lucky for us, he had more than a bit of con and cunning to go along with his sense of humor. One day, a shipment of frozen pork arrived with the shipment of provisions. Since it took about four hours to make it from Manila to Corregidor, the pork was half thawed by the time we laid our hands on it. Seizing the opportunity, Monahan pressed the pork sides with his thumb while expounding on the danger of trichinosis to the Japanese mess sergeant. He repeated the process driving bigger holes into the sides of the pork and gravely recommended against serving the pork to his troops. I didn't know whether the sergeant was gullible or whether Monahan had done that great a con job on him. Anyway, the sergeant ordered Monahan to get rid of the pork presumed to be bad. Monahan quickly complied, not by disposing of the huge slabs of pork but by loading the entire shipment onto our truck. When we got back to the motor pool, we hastily stored the pork sides in a freezer unit that we had previously scrounged up and repaired for our own use. It was a significant addition to our larder and again, a tribute to the ingenuity of our marines. As usual, Sergeant Nolan outdid himself in laying out variations of pork for our dinner enjoyment.

My assignment had unexpected advantages. For example, the Japanese garrison commander was very fond of seafood and he demanded that it be provided fresh every day for his dinner. Three Filipino fishermen were therefore retained at Corregidor to indulge his passion for that bit of luxury. One of my jobs was to provide transportation for the fishermen to various sites on the island to do their daily fishing. They were an amiable lot with no particular attachment to the cause of the Rising Sun and so we developed a "special" understanding that allowed me to pick out the most sizable fish and lobsters for our little unit. They were aware that it was going to the Americans and had no qualms about helping us out. At least it appeared that way. Moreover, the usual catch was about two or three lobsters a day so at least twice a week, I took two lobsters back to the motor pool.

Often, Sergeant Nolan prepared lobsters for the Japanese sergeant and superior private assigned to oversee the motor pool. This was in return for their kindness. They, in turn, shared their ration of beer, cigarettes, and candies with us. The two of them were exceptional individuals. They saw us as human beings caught in unfortunate circumstances, and although there was a limit to how far they could go to be kind to us, we recognized their generosity as being genuine. For the first time since the fighting began in the Philippines, we were able to see that not all Japanese soldiers were the same. The two of them opened our eyes to their humanistic inclinations, which was quite obvious in spite of the war.

On the other hand, the noncommissioned officer in charge of our overseers constantly demanded the impossible of both of them and often slapped the sergeant for being too lax in his treatment of us. The junior sergeant who persisted in treating us decently was much younger. He was a reservist and since he had no intention of making the military his career, he did nothing to ingratiate himself with the senior noncommissioned officer. He always kept his relationship with him on a formal and correct level. We couldn't help but feel very sorry for him and his plight as a much maligned underling of the sergeant major.

The sergeant major was an overbearing individual who reveled in exercising power and in enjoying the perquisites of a senior noncommissioned officer. Reaching the position of the highest noncommissioned officer was considered quite an honor in the Japanese Army, and he struck me as a calculating opportunist who had done everything in his power to get to that position.

His pride and joy on Corregidor was a Harley Davidson motorcycle that once belonged to the Corps of U.S. Military Police. It was pretty well banged up when he first spotted it during a routine tour of the island. True to his nature, he ordered us to haul the motorcycle back to the motor pool and have it running again within a week. Fortunately for us, we had in Sergeant Smith, an outstanding auto mechanic with years of experience at a General Motors plant back in the States. He had to rely on makeshift parts and work through several nights to get the motorcycle running again, but he somehow succeeded in meeting the deadline. The sergeant was obviously smitten by the machine and we were willing to bet that if he had a wife vying for his affections, she probably would have lost to the motorcycle.

Day after day we watched him as his proficiency with the motorcycle increased. Every improvement was accompanied by an obvious surge of pride that quickly showed up on his face. Eventually, we decided that he was due for a good scare. We noticed that he had adopted the daily ritual of inspecting all of the outposts on Corregidor on his Harley Davidson. So one day we filled his Harley Davidson with 100 percent pure ether and tested it. We thought it worked magnificently for our needs. The motorcycle ran with a pronounced zip that would surely take the sergeant major by surprise—at least we were hoping that it would.

At the usual time, he showed up for his Harley. To allay any suspicion, we did not gather around him. Instead, we peered curiously from our individual vantage points to see what would happen. He kick started it, adjusted himself on the seat, and then gunned the machine for all it was worth. He took off like a P-40, leaving us in a wake of dust. He seemed startled and was last seen hanging on for dear life as he roared down a winding highway called Middleway Road that was on a downward incline. He quickly disappeared from our line of sight. We thought it was hilariously funny at first but we were soon horrified by the possibility that he may have crashed. In that case, we would all be in trouble.

About an hour later, we heard him returning and we braced for the worst possible consequence. Contrary to our expectations, he came back with a grin that stretched from ear to ear. He was obviously delighted with the performance of the motorcycle and announced that forthwith, he expected the Harley to be fueled with nothing but high-octane fuel.

The joke was on us. We were also saddled with the problem of keeping adequate supplies of ether for his motorcycle. It meant looking around at the hospital and all known field dispensaries for new sources of ether. Fortunately, the major and the battalion that he commanded on the island were soon relieved of garrison duty by a company of troops commanded by a lieutenant.

The lieutenant and his troops were primarily reservists, so we expected life to take a turn for the better on Corregidor. We at least expected the troops to be less harsh in their treatment of the POWs.

One day, the lieutenant was called to the 16th Division Headquarters at Fort Stotsenberg, the location of Clark Air Base. Upon his return I was summoned to his office where he informed me that I would be leaving Corregidor in a day or two for Fort Stotsenberg. He seemed pleasant enough and he tried to reassure me about the move. However, the only information that he was willing to divulge to me was that division headquarters had worked out plans that would be "to my advantage." I had no idea what he meant by that. I could only pray for the best. At the same time, I was saddened by the prospect of leaving a great bunch of guys at the motor pool.

Two days later, I was escorted by a corporal to Fort Stotsenberg, a trip that was made via the Bataan Peninsula. Little did I realize what awaited me at that destination.

Chapter 9

INTO THE HELLHOLE

The trip to Fort Stotsenberg via Bataan was depressing. From the vantage point of the vehicle in which I was riding, the view was fleeting, but I could still see the carnage of war stretched as far as the eye could see. The burned remains of tanks, trucks, sedans, weapons of every description, helmets, knapsacks, spent casings and cartridges, all symbols of strength and invincibility when they were arrayed in battle readiness prior to the outbreak of the war, now lay scattered in disarray. There were nothing but scenes of abject desolation.

It was just as well that my view was obscured. In my emotional state, I was better served by a retreat into denial. I knew all along that it would never be easy to accept defeat in battle and that it would be even tougher to be objective about it even with all the evidence at hand. But nonetheless, the first glimpse of the downside of war was both disheartening and disconcerting.

For the rest of the trip, I alternated between moments of consciousness and sleep as monotony and sounds of the whirring engine put me into a stupor. A sudden lurch of our vehicle as it swerved to avoid something strewn on the highway suddenly shook me back

129

into reality. What had been friendly territory not too long ago was now enemy territory and I was in enemy hands. For some reason I thought about the adage that an army must learn to cope with defeat in battle if it is to ultimately achieve greatness. The war was still on and as small as my role was in the whole scheme of things, I still had a job to do.

The look on the face of the corporal escorting me ranged from the morose to sullen withdrawal. It was obvious that he preferred not to communicate with me. To while the time away, I sat there in the vehicle wondering what he was thinking behind his mask of feigned impassiveness. But a grunt, snort, or brusque gesture was all that I could get out of him. I was curious to know whether his demeanor was a Japanese aversion to unfamiliar people and situations or his way of showing contempt for an enemy soldier.

The idle musing that occupied me during the last phase of the ride to Fort Stotsenberg was not all in vain. By the time we got to the fort, I was secure in my thoughts and I was ready to face whatever awaited me. I was fortunate to have snapped out of my earlier stupor because what the lieutenant at Corregidor had said to me about "plans for my benefit" was anything but that. I was being set up and the Kempeitai was again licking its chops to get a hold of me.

As soon as I arrived at Fort Stotsenberg, I was deposited in a jail cell measuring about six feet square. During my three days of confinement in the cell, my meals consisted of leftovers from what the guards had been fed. They made it a point to leave me very little to eat. On the fourth day, I was subjected to intense interrogation by a Kempeitai sergeant detailed to 16th Division Headquarters. He charged me with treasonable actions against the Japanese military and he informed me that he would be escorting me to Manila for further interrogation at 14th Army Headquarters.

Upon arriving in Manila, I was taken to the old Bilibid Prison, a section of which was utilized as a military prison of Japanese soldiers and political prisoners from other countries. As we drove up the driveway to the entrance of the prison I had only a brief glimpse of the structure. A part of the facade reminded me of a fortress taken right out of the movie *Beau Geste*. Only, this was not a fortress. It was a prison and it had a forbidding look that worried me as I was escorted in by the sergeant.

I was placed in a cell with a group of Japanese soldiers charged variously with crimes ranging from rape and murder to desertion. I prepared myself for the worst. My own impression of prison life was heavily colored by what I had seen in the movies. But like so many things about the Japanese, I found that they did things quite differently.

In the first place, there was no animosity or overt acts of hostility directed at me when I entered the cell to which I was assigned. That was probably because as prisoners, we were all in the same boat, and also, as I was to learn later on, they thought I was a former Japanese civilian employee of the Japanese Army. My cellmates made no attempt to grill me about my background.

The other surprise was the weight of Japanese custom. Like Japanese society in general, there was an unspoken concern for form and custom that had to be observed even in prison. For example, there was a cell leader determined on the basis of seniority. Naturally, seniority accrued to those with the longest prison term. Upon arrival, each newcomer to the cell was required to to present himself in front of the cell leader in a formally prescribed Japanese manner. The newcomer was also required to bow and speak using the language and terms regarded as appropriate to the occasion to introduce himself and to state the reason for his confinement. I summoned up as much as I had learned in school about such matters to go through the ritual. What I did was apparently adequate for the occasion.

In other words, conformity began within the cell group and it was enforced not by physical coercion as in so many American prisons today but by a set of customs. Moreover, each cell leader was required to conduct himself according to the highest standards of leadership. Failure to do so could result in removal and in the worst case, a loss of face.

Following the introduction, the newcomer of the cell was customarily assigned to cater to the needs of the cell leader. As the newest member of the cell, I was required to do all of his personal laundry and to turn over whatever portion of my daily food ration he so desired. As the junior member of the cell, I performed those duties for about eight months.

There were eight people in a cell that measured about eight feet by twelve feet. The cells were cramped and when we lay down to sleep at night on the straw mats that they furnished each of us, there was hardly any room to move around. The straw mats were only about two-and-a-half to three feet long so when we slept on them, they only protected about half of our bodies from the concrete floor. Each man was also furnished one blanket. It goes without saying that there was absolutely no privacy.

The toilet in our cell was a tiny wooden bench with a hole cut in it. It reminded me of a child's potty seat. The only way to preserve a modicum of privacy when using the toilet was to fashion a make-shift screen around oneself with the tiny mat. There was no flushing mechanism. There was only the flow of water in the ditch under us. If the water was flowing, it was all right. If not, the smell was something awful.

The cell contained a small water faucet that we used to wash ourselves and our clothing.

At the epicenter of the prison complex was a huge circular building with a high wall bisecting it. Perched at the top of the building was a watchtower. There were other inner walls that divided the huge compound into three or four parts. All that I was familiar with was the side for Japanese and other Asian prisoners. I also heard that there was a separate compound for Americans and other Westerners. Because of the wall, we were not able to see anything on the other side of the compound.

Our daily routine consisted of reveille at 6:00 A.M. followed by roll call and calisthenics prior to breakfast. We used U.S. Army mess kits to eat our meals, and rice mixed with turnips was a common part of our spare diet. We were also given what amounted to about a cup of soup, which was ladled into our canteen cups. It tasted like a salt-based soup with a few slices of seasoned vegetables in the broth, if one could call it that. Meals were taken at the command of the guard on duty and when he commanded us to "cease eating," we were all required to stop eating regardless of whether we were finished or not. Needless to say, we all ate fast, no matter what they served.

132

The rest of the day was spent either on a work detail or in interrogation by members of the Kempeitai.

My interrogator was a sergeant major. For interrogation I was taken to a small bungalow located next to a supply shack. The interrogations were intense and were conducted in three-hour segments every day over a ten-day stretch. He advised me at the outset that I was being charged with committing treason and that it was his responsibility to set the record straight on my real relationship to the U.S. military.

I sensed trouble from the first day that I entered Bilibid Prison. To my grave dismay, I learned that there were about three hundred prisoners incarcerated there for allowing themselves to become prisoners of the U.S. Army. They were recovered by the Japanese forces after the fall of Bataan but were not allowed to return to duty. All were court-martialed and those who had the misfortune to be found guilty were sentenced to prison terms ranging from five years to life in Bilibid Prison. All of the rules governing the handling of soldiers captured by enemy forces were specified in the Japanese Code of Military Conduct. This meant that there would be a good chance that I would be running into some of the prisoners that I had interrogated in Bataan. It didn't take long for my worst fears to be confirmed.

During the calisthenics break on my first day at Bilibid, several of the prisoners approached me and asked, "Aren't you Sergeant Sakakida who interrogated us on Bataan?" I walked away without replying but I felt trapped. My response was a reflex mechanism honed to hair-trigger sensitivity by fear. I was hoping that the prisoners who had recognized me would somehow disappear.

When the interrogations began for me, I learned that the prisoners had indeed identified me as the noncommissioned officer on the American side who had interrogated them when they were in American hands. The sergeant demanded to know my rank in the U.S. military and all about my recruitment into U.S. military intelligence. I continued to deny my military status and I repeated the same story that I had provided the Kempeitai colonel who interrogated me on Corregidor.

The sergeant was unmoved by my story and at one point in the

133

interrogation, he called in several of the former POWs to let me hear what they had to say about the chevrons that I wore on the sleeves of my uniform. In my presence, they reported that when they saw me, I was wearing the uniform of either a staff or tech sergeant.

The sergeant turned to me and said, "What do you say to that?"

My reply was that I was hurriedly evacuated by the U.S. military from Manila to Bataan and then on to Corregidor. In the rush, I had no time to pack and all I had was what I had on when I left Manila. I told him that because of that, on Bataan I had no change of clothes whatsoever. And because my clothes were so filthy, some NCOs in G2 offered to lend me their spare uniforms while my civilian clothes were being laundered. The sergeant was still skeptical and decided at that point to resort to more drastic measures. He was determined to get the confession that he wanted out of me.

I lied to my interrogators and I didn't like lying even while I was being tortured. Lying went against something of fundamental value that I was taught at home, in the classroom, and by my religious teachers. The orthodoxy that defined my military responsibilities was my only hedge against self-doubt. I felt that right or wrong, I had to do whatever it took to continue on with my mission. I saw it as a matter of duty as the interrogation took on a violent turn. From then on, I was put through a series of torture treatments and incessant beatings.

He began by having my hands tied behind my back and stringing me up to a rope that had been thrown over a rafter in the interrogation room. I was kept dangling with my toes just barely off of the floor. The pain was excruciating and after a time, it felt as if my arms were being torn out of my shoulder sockets. All the while, he kept asking me, "What is your true military rank?" I kept denying that I was part of the military. Soon the pain reached a point at which I thought I would have to scream but the persistent questioning raised my blood to the boiling point and all of a sudden the rage that welled up inside of me came on like some sort of divine intercession. Sweat poured out of my body and I was enraged as I had never ever been before in my life and suddenly, the overriding pain was diminished to a level where my will to resist could be kept intact.

I don't know how my ravaged mind and body were able to mus-

ter the burst of spirituality that saved me from going over the edge
but for that, I shall be eternally grateful. It gave me mental leverage
and I vowed with a rage bordering on madness that I would not
succumb to torture. By then, I knew that he would have to kill me
or somehow separate me from my senses to get me to capitulate.
Suddenly, I felt as if I was in control of myself. The Japanese have
always been known for their stoic acceptance of fate even in the face
of death. They refer to it as a capacity for *gaman*, or endurance,
something that my parents and Buddhist teachers taught me as I
was growing up in Hawaii. As early as I could remember, we were
taught that it was shameful to cry when faced with physical pain,
and I was determined to show him that on that score, I was just as
Japanese as he was. I stared him right in his eyes. I also vowed that
if I ever survived the war, I would someday hunt him down. At that
moment, I felt that I could kill him.

Realizing that he was not getting his way with me, he decided to
push the torture up a notch. He had some men strip me of my
clothing until I was stark naked. He still kept me dangling from the
rafters as he systematically took a lighted cigarette to inflict burns
on me. He started in the area of my thighs. As the days went on, he
went up to the area of my abdomen before finally getting to my
genitals, hoping all along that I would crack. The pain, added to the
pain in my arms that already felt as if they were dislocated, was
indescribable. I was subjected to the same torture day after day.
There were times when I felt like screaming as loud as I could but I
refused to give them even that satisfaction. After a while, I began to
lapse into a state of extreme nausea compounded by the smell of
burning flesh—my own.

To this day, I don't know how I endured the ordeal. Perhaps it
was my Buddhist upbringing that made me turn inward, looking for
inner strength to counter the pain that had already reached an almost unbearable level. Fortunately, my rebelliousness and Buddhist
faith held me in good stead. If I was enraged during the early stages
of torture, I was by then, delivered to a state of incandescent fury,
particularly as he buried the cigarette into my penis. That was the
last straw and I knew that in my state of indescribable rage, my
torturer was not about to break the steel-like clamp on my nerves. I

felt as if I had entered a dark tunnel where the light at the end was visible only to me. Today, I can count about thirty to forty scars resulting from the ordeal.

In the days that followed, the cigarette burns inflicted on me became infected. My penis was covered with pus and rendered raw by the constant rubbing inflicted on it by my coarse prison trousers. The irritation and discomfort accompanying every movement was excruciating—physically and mentally. At night, as I slept, the blood and pus would coagulate and stick to my trousers, leaving freshly exposed flesh to cope with the following morning.

Occasionally, a huge fifty-gallon drum filled with clean hot water would be brought into the prison grounds to allow prisoners to bathe. The order in which the prisoners were allowed to bathe was determined by numbers that were assigned to everyone. So those who got to bathe early enjoyed the luxury of clean, hot water. The water in the drum was never changed, so after a few soakings the water turned noticeably murky. Pretty soon the surface was covered with a layer of unsightly froth and body oil. My number was 207 so I decided not to bathe to keep my burns from getting even more infected. When my turn arrived, however, I was ordered into the drum of filthy water. The water by then looked like black coffee and the surface of the water was covered with what can best be described as crud. The filthy water and an instinctive fear of aggravating my burn wounds made me blanch but I had no choice but to immerse myself in it. I prayed for the best as I emerged from my "bath." The cigarette burns did not improve. In fact, they took a turn for the worse, so I was finally granted permission to go to the dispensary for treatment.

At the dispensary, the medic asked me how it all happened. I told him that it all stemmed from the cigarette burns inflicted on me during my interrogation.

Shrugging in disgust, he turned to me and said, "Do you expect me to believe that?"

"Yes sir," I replied. Instead of showing sympathy for my wounds, which were oozing with infection by then, he knocked me against the wall of the dispensary. I was more shocked than upset at first. I certainly didn't expect that kind of treatment from a medic. But there I was, sprawled on the floor.

Eyes flashing with contempt, he said, "You're a carrier of venereal disease. How dare you blame the Japanese military for your indiscretions?"

He accused me of lying, "just like an American," even though he probably never ever met an American before. My treatment consisted of no treatment, only further abuse. Thereupon, my only recourse was self-administered treatment. I washed my penis and the other cigarette inflicted wounds with plain water several times a day. Miraculously, they eventually healed, but today I carry my own version of an "imperial household crest" firmly scarred on my penis. It is hardly a work of art.

During the ten-day stretch with the Kempeitai sergeant, I was subjected to a variety of other tortures and endless beatings. It culminated with them putting a water hose into my mouth to pump me full of water until I felt as if I would burst. The interrogation ended when they were sure that I wouldn't talk.

Today, it hurts just to talk about the torture. Suffice it to say, I survived without breaking or confessing.

Once the sergeant's interrogation was over with, I was called by a captain assigned to the judge advocate general's office under Headquarters, 14th Army, which exercised overall command and control over the Japanese forces in the Philippines. He again went over everything covered in the sergeant's investigation report on me as well as the report submitted to the 14th Army by the colonel who interviewed me on Corregidor. He made it a point to go over every issue again.

Since the charge being leveled at me was treason, it was the captain's responsibility to clarify my status as a dual citizen. He questioned me about my parental origins and he informed me that he would have the family register of the Sakakida clan checked to determine my status. The captain did not resort to physical abuse. He accorded me the courtesy of an invitation to take a tea break with him and he was kind enough to furnish me with cigarettes throughout the interrogation.

Two weeks after his initial interrogation, I was once again summoned by the captain to his office. He asked me whether I was aware of the fact that my Japanese citizenship had been renounced just prior to the war and that made me a non-Japanese. However, he informed me that the Japanese military still interpreted my past actions to be conduct in support of the enemy side and therefore hostile to the Japanese cause. One key point, as far as they were concerned was that I was born of Japanese parentage, which made me liable to the charge of treason. Thus, I was still liable to stand trial.

What he had to do apparently was buttress the legal basis of their arguments to press their case. He therefore focused on the conditions surrounding the renunciation of my citizenship. He pressed me again so I told him that my mother was of the old school of thought and that since I had left home over her objections, she disowned me by striking my name from the family register. He accepted that as a logical reason and said that I would be hearing from him later on. It all depended on the decision of army headquarters on the final disposition of my case.

There were an average of two trials a month conducted by the Japanese Military Court. I was transported to court on three different occasions, but I was always returned to prison without being tried. It was probably all part of a policy of harassment, which I could do nothing about, so I bided my time quietly.

In the meantime, I was summoned to the prison director's office one day, and to my surprise, sitting in the office was the lieutenant who had accompanied us back on the boat from Cabcaben after General Wainwright had his meeting with General Homma. This time, however, he was dressed in civilian clothes. He was the one who had heard about my problems at the Nippon Club and had tried to console me with sympathetic accounts of how concerned the residents at the club had been about my ultimate fate. He told me that he too was concerned about me but that he was prevented from inquiring about me because of the press of his military duties. He went on to explain that he was now out of military service and was working for a Japanese industrial firm in Manila and that this was his first opportunity to pay me a visit. Actually, the lieutenant was a counterintelligence officer operating under civilian cover and I went out of my way to convince him that I believed what he was telling me.

Soon after the lieutenant's visit, I was called by a major who was the lieutenant's superior and also commander of the Special Activities Unit of G2, 14th Army Headquarters. He brought along some American-brand cigarettes and Japanese pastries and insisted that I help myself to them. I sensed something in the making when he began to ask me whether I missed Hawaii and the members of my family. It seemed like a ridiculous question to ask of a prisoner of war who was being accused of treason and undergoing all kinds of privation and torture. But I was enjoying the cigarettes and pastries too much to put an end to the visit. As long as I was free to help myself to those wondrous treats, I was not about to terminate his visit. I played along. I kept waiting for his pitch but it never came during the first visit.

Thereafter, his visits became frequent and I kept enjoying the treats. Finally, in December 1942, he asked me whether I would like to return to Hawaii if it could be arranged. I jokingly replied in the affirmative, but I quickly added, "It's impossible you know, after all, there's a war on." Then came the pitch. He advised me of a Japanese military plan being hatched to surreptitiously put a man on shore in Hawaii using a submarine. The man they had in mind for the plan was me. Obviously, I was not about to betray America, but at the same time, I was not sure what exactly they were up to so I strung things out by saying that I would have to think about it. After his initial pitch, he visited me three more times. Each time he asked me about the offer and each time, I replied that I had not made up my mind yet. After that, his visits ended and thus ended my brief access to cigarettes and pastries. He had apparently given up on me.

After a time, my prison activities changed. They started giving me "spiritual training." To undergo spiritual training, I was taken to the inner courtyard adjoining the prison director's office. The courtyard has always been an integral part of Asian architecture. It has always provided a link between a dwelling or office and a part of the natural environment surrounding it. So I expected to find a courtyard that was far more appealing than what I found.

The prison director's office courtyard was neat but spare and un-

139

adorned. Jails have a way of making everything look bleak. Nevertheless, after sitting behind bars for so long, there was a serenity about the place that I liked. Perhaps that was the whole idea, to get me to think things through from another angle.

On every occasion, I was given a gallon container and told to pick up the tiny pebbles covering the courtyard one by one until the container was full. I started from one end of the courtyard and worked across to the opposite end. Each time I finished filling the container, the guard took it and scattered the pebbles back over the courtyard. I would then be ordered to repeat the process. So I did, over and over again. That was the extent of my spiritual training. I was told that it was all part of a spiritual exercise to cleanse me of my "Yankee spirit."

They were wrong. All the torture and beating did not dampen my Yankee spirit and whatever spirit it was that was fueling my resistance. They not only rekindled that spirit in prison; they set it on fire.

Gathering pebbles was repetitive and boring at first but it was also therapeutic. It was also a whole lot better than being beaten. For the first time in a long while, I had the luxury of contemplation rather than being riveted to concerns about being unmasked every waking minute of the day. I began to notice the difference in the shape and character of each pebble that I handled. I began to see unvarnished beauty in places and things that I had never stopped to examine with care before. Unwittingly the artistically unschooled mind of a young soldier began to take shape. Years later, it would lead to an awareness and appreciation of Japanese folk art that persists to this very day. The so-called spiritual indoctrination was not all that bad, although I was too young and impressionable to really appreciate it at that time. Moreover, I was still a POW with a cloud hanging over my head and I had no idea what fate awaited me. Every time I was led back to my prison cell, I was back to square one.

Chapter 10

FAREWELL TO BILIBID

The so-called spiritual training and torture sessions were followed by a period of standard prison chores. However, being under suspicion, I could hardly expect even an ordinary assignment to be free of harassment. They assigned me to a chore that I personally found annoying. As part of my new duties, I had to clean the latrines used by the prison director and guards.

The relationship between work on spiritual training and the pits of human excrement, if there was any significance intended, was lost on me. The only thing that sunk into my awareness as I cleaned the latrines was the stench, which was overwhelming. Yet, as disagreeable as the work was, I made it a point not to allow my captors to think that I was upset. I was not about to give them any kind of satisfaction. I did the best job that I could under the circumstances, giving the latrines a thorough cleaning. One thing they couldn't hold against me was failing to do a good job. I was also careful not to betray any untoward emotions to my captors. The Japanese are good at that but I figured, so was I.

It was during this period that I had a dream one night that was, at first blush, too much like wishful thinking. It had been a night of fitful sleep and late into the night I thought I heard a voice telling me that my confinement in prison was about to end. I awoke confused and wet with perspiration. Looking around me, I realized that nothing had changed, and the only sound was the snoring of my fellow inmates. It was just a dream, and as I lay there in the darkness, I took comfort from the fact that I had survived to this point. But that dream was prophetic.

Two days later, on 11 February 1943, I was summoned to the prison director's office. It was the day of *Kingensetsu*, otherwise known as Empire Day or National Foundation Day. When I got to the office, I was ordered to change into the clothing that I had worn when I first arrived at the prison. Having done that, I was then told that I was to be escorted to 14th Army Headquarters. They handed me my belongings, which, to my delight, included my treasured gold watch.

My status had changed, but to what? Suspicion welled up as they handcuffed me and led me to a waiting car. Our destination was a three-story government building. It was the former Philippine Ministry of Agriculture building.

The office staff consisted of three officers, one typist, four civil servants, one local-hire woman, whose sole job appeared to be to serve tea to the office staff, and one civilian security officer. The staff was commanded by a diminutive colonel who looked to be barely five feet tall. He made up for short stature with an exaggerated strut and manner bordering on arrogance. As I stood at attention wearing my handcuffs, he cast a steely glance at me. He then went about sizing me up from head to toe. If he had a point to make, he was obviously in no hurry to get to it. He got up and strolled around me, not saying a word and looking as stern as he possibly could. I stood there, worried, wondering what was coming. He eventually returned to his seat behind a massive desk before facing me again. He continued to fix me in a cold stare. Finally he spoke: through the grace and magnanimity of the Japanese Imperial Army, the treason charges against me were being dropped, and, henceforth, I was to serve as the interpreter for his office.

For a minute, I was speechless. I didn't know whether to feel relieved or grateful. There were just too many things to sort out in

142

that one brief moment after his unexpected announcement. I didn't even stop to think whether protocol demanded that I thank him. All I could blurt out was, "As of when, sir?" "Right now!" he replied without hesitation.

Later I learned that the death sentence that the colonel had wished for me was overturned by General Wachi, chief of staff of 14th Army Headquarters. He reached his decision after reading the results of the investigation. Wachi's reasoning, according to my source, was that the judge advocate's office would probably be better off using my bilingual capability, which was in short supply. He felt that taking my life would be easy enough, but it was important for them to use me prior to eliminating me.

In 1949, when I was stationed in Tokyo with the U.S. Air Force Office of Special Investigation, General Wachi paid an unannounced visit to my office. During his visit, we reminisced about our days in the Philippines. He did not seem overly surprised to see me. My presence in uniform must have confirmed the suspicion of many on his staff that I was connected with the U.S. military in the Philippines, but the fact was, they had no substantiating proof.

Apparently, there was also an element of compassion in his decision to overrule the death sentence ordered by the judge advocate general. He noticed that my parents originated from Hiroshima Prefecture, which also happened to be his home. He felt that he would have been hard put to reconcile his feelings with that of my aged mother should she have learned that I was executed by the Japanese military. General Wachi struck me as a very honorable man and I was fortunate to be favored by his sense of compassion.

Once I got over the shock of being cleared of the charge of treason, I was able to sort out my own thoughts. I would now be able to get back into intelligence collection as advised by Colonel Pugh, and one thing was for sure: I did not want to serve as an interpreter for the Japanese. What I feared most was the possibility of compromising the safety of American soldiers captured by the Japanese. I had to think of some way to get out of my predicament.

I told the colonel that it was a relief to have the treason charge behind me. I was a victim of circumstances, I said, and therefore innocent of the charges leveled against me.

143

I asked him, "What if I should somehow fall into American hands? What if they charge me with treason for interrogating American prisoners?" I implored him to think of the torture I'd received from his own people and imagine what the Americans would do to me. I even surprised myself at the tone of my remarks. But I was no longer a naive kid who had been roped into this mission. My survival was at stake and I felt I had a case to make. I tried to convince him that the reason the American forces were able to utilize my linguistic skills was that I was an American citizen.

"As an American citizen, I had no choice but to serve!" I literally shouted. "Sure, maybe charging me with treason against Japan and putting me in prison was a mistake, but what about all the torture you put me through? Now you're asking me to turn around and possibly commit treason against the United States. Who is going to stand up for me if the tables are turned?"

I apologized for the outburst, which seemed to surprise everyone. The people working in there were all educated and intelligent and seemed to understand my predicament when I went on to say that I was sick and tired of being buffeted around like a piece of driftwood in some turbulent ocean current helplessly waiting to be cast ashore somewhere with no hope of controlling my fate.

The colonel was obviously taken by surprise. He blinked, betraying a perceptible slip in the unwavering look of toughness he maintained as he fixed me with that stare. Somehow, I sensed a vein of compassion as I pressed my argument, but he had his orders and he was not about to budge. Moreover, his self-esteem was at stake, and I had to admit, he was tough.

After hearing me out, he cleared his throat, looked me straight in the eyes and said directly, "Nothing you say will alter the decision of the Japanese military command." He added that dropping the treason charge was "a benevolent act" bestowed on the occasion of National Foundation Day and that I should accept the magnanimous gesture with "due humility."

I was in for another surprise. "Henceforth," he announced, "you will be staying at my quarters." He had his reasons for keeping me near him. First and foremost, he didn't trust me and he wanted close supervisory control over me. Second, he apparently thought it would be handy to have an English-speaking person with him since his home was located in a Filipino community.

I stood in the office feeling isolated all over again and wondering what sort of gut-wrenching roller coaster ride I was in for this time. I was no longer behind bars but we were at war and I could be accused of any kind of trumped-up charge at any time.

The colonel occupied a huge home located in the suburb of Manila called Pasay. The home bore no resemblance to Japanese homes or to the Nipa huts that the Filipino families occupied. The home was formerly occupied by the manager of the Standard Oil Company. It was of a Spanish architecture in the tropical style beloved by foreign business community leaders in prewar Manila. Upstairs, it had a huge living-dining room surrounded by a kitchen and six other rooms. Downstairs was a large garage, a covered patio, and four more rooms. The home was fully furnished and well appointed for gracious living. The flooring, bannisters, and furniture were of hardwood polished to a high sheen. The home was kept immaculately clean at all times by the colonel's household staff. A Filipino gardener kept the huge lawn and garden surrounding the home looking luxuriant and neatly trimmed. Meals were prepared by a cook, and a chauffeur drove the American-made car. Senior officers of the Japanese occupation forces in the Philippines were accorded such living quarters throughout Manila.

The colonel occupied the master bedroom on the second floor. I occupied a room on the first floor with his chauffeur, houseboy, and cook. My introduction to my roommates was cool, at best. However, they attempted a show of civility toward me in front of the colonel. All three of them had been brought over from Taiwan and it was easy to understand their resentment so I let it pass. After all, I had a Japanese name and they probably had no love for the Japanese who were occupying Taiwan, and more likely than not, they had been brought to the Philippines against their will. I was also intruding upon their meager privacy, and it was quite evident that they didn't like being seen by others as mere servants.

As time went on, our relations did not improve at all. They made it a point to let me know that I was unwelcome. They found out that I was a prisoner, which, in their eyes, put my status in the

145

household a cut below theirs. As servants who had been stepped on and exploited, they seemed to relish the opportunity to do the same to someone below them.

I endured their thinly veiled taunts, slights, and overbearing arrogance for about a month. By then I knew how the household was organized and operated. "Enough is enough," I said to myself and decided that it was safe to take matters into my own hands. The one thing they seemed to respect was force, so I slapped them around for starters. I took it to each of them and made it clear that henceforth, they were to listen to me and not vice versa. I also checked out all of the skeletons in the closet so that I had something to use against each of them in case they tried to turn the colonel against me. I managed to turn them around but I was not naive enough to let my guard down. I was certain that they would be waiting to take revenge on me. This was a cat and mouse game that I had to be aware of at all times.

The colonel's home was a storehouse of foreign liquors, cigarettes, American canned goods, and other fine consumer products that were unavailable in local markets. All of the items were confiscated by the Japanese Army when it took Manila and they were delivered in the form of monthly rations to the colonel's quarters. The bulk of the canned goods were from the U.S. Quartermaster Corps warehouses.

The colonel dined alone at night in a huge dining room. He was served a drink or two with his dinner but he rarely exceeded his nightly intake of liquor beyond that. Moreover, he was a nonsmoker so his cache of cigarettes and liquor grew proportionately larger every month. Never once did he offer us anything from his collection, which confirmed my guess that he was stingy.

One evening, during the colonel's absence, I snuck into his bedroom and discovered cartons of American cigarettes and other goods crammed into his closet. I purloined two cartons of my favorite brand, Camels, from his vast collection. My rationale was that I had more right than he had to enjoy American cigarettes that were confiscated from U.S. military warehouses.

Once I had the cigarettes in hand, I had to find some place to smoke them. American cigarettes were easily distinguishable from Filipino and Japanese cigarettes by their smell so I took to smoking them in the bathroom. By then, cigarette smoking was no longer just a habit. It was a terrible addiction. The nicotine hook, worsened by an underlying obsession borne of months and months of pain, worry, and deprivation was just too much for me to cope with. I just had to smoke. Every time I stepped into the bathroom to have a Camel, I found myself sucking and inhaling with such fervor that it made me wonder whether it was really me. Finally, I had to force myself to calm down.

Life had taken a turn for the better in many ways. I was not being tortured, I was eating and sleeping regularly, and I was even smoking American cigarettes. But I was still under suspicion and confinement. I had to find some way to get back to my military duties.

Whenever the opportunity presented itself, I volunteered to remain at the office after hours to assist the duty officer of the judge advocate directorate with various chores. This gave me the opportunity to browse around the office and to determine the location of their classified documents. The duty officer normally took a thirty-minute security check break every three hours and that gave me sufficient time to read over any classified documents that happened to be left unattended on his desk.

One day, I was told by the warrant officer that the deputy assistant chief of staff, G2, wanted to see me immediately. I reported to his office and knocked on his door. I heard a booming voice reply, "Enter!" so I complied. I was taken aback to see two majors and the lieutenant in civilian clothes from counterintelligence as well. The major who summoned me pointed a finger at me immediately and said, "Sakakida, you are a sergeant in the U.S. Army!" It caught me by surprise and I felt a cold chill go up and down my spine, as I began to ponder the possibility that perhaps my time was finally up. But I quickly regained my composure and mustered a look of complete innocence to deny his accusation. I was determined to stick to my denial as long as I could, although deep down inside of me I began to think that sooner or later, my true military identity would become known to them. The incessant interrogations and beatings had begun to wear down my armor of resistance but I still wanted to stick to my cover story.

Again, I was bombarded with questions from all sides in the major's office but I was adamant in emphasizing that if I were in the military, I would not have accompanied the members of the Japanese community into the Japanese evacuation center. I told them that it would have been much better for me to be imprisoned with the rest of the American POWs than stay with the Japanese prisoners. They relented and I was dismissed to return to duty in the office, but I was told to expect to be called back for further questioning.

Obviously, I was still under a cloud of suspicion and thereafter, I was doubly careful about everything I did or said in the compound. Meanwhile, there were all sorts of seemingly innocuous requests made of me to trip me up. For example, one day, the warrant officer handed me a U.S. Army .45 caliber automatic and ordered me to clean it. I was going to fieldstrip the weapon but sensed that it might be a trap. So I busied myself oiling and rubbing down the weapon without disassembling a single part. When I took the weapon back to him, he inspected the barrel and caustically reprimanded me for not fieldstripping it and for doing a sloppy job. I told him that I had never fieldstripped a weapon before but that if he would teach me how to do it, I would be glad to clean it again. Evidently, he was also unfamiliar with the weapon and he said to me, "Well, I'm busy and this will have to do for now."

Thereafter, I lived as if I were on borrowed time. I lived for each day and never let my hopes range beyond that. I prepared myself for the eventuality that they might still be able to expose, identify, and execute me as an enemy spy. At that point, all of my efforts would have been in vain and I was not about to let that happen. At least not yet.

I also decided to exploit every opportunity to further my mission as long as I could go on undetected. I was determined not to do anything rash and to weigh each opportunity from every conceivable angle. It was time to do something positive instead of being on the defensive.

One facet of Japanese military life that I noticed very distinctly was that rank had its privileges. It was, of course, a feature common to military organizations all over the world. But I thought that it was particularly pronounced in the Japanese Army. I had to make a move and one thought that occurred to me was the uniform and rank as passports to denied areas. Since I was only twenty-one years old, I would not be able to impersonate a captain or field-grade officer but I was sure that I could pass as an officer candidate if I could find the right uniform to do it in.

I began to watch for opportunities. I first began to look for the right insignia. Under the Japanese military system, officer candidate trainees had cherry blossoms on top of the sergeant major's insignia as a distinguishing feature. In the military pecking order, the officer candidate enjoyed the privileges of a commissioned officer but stood junior in authority to the second lieutenant.

In the judge advocate's office where I was occasionally assigned was an officer candidate on assignment who happened to be about my age. He wore glasses and cut quite a handsome figure. Because of his good looks and carefree nature, he was always out during off-duty hours enjoying the pleasures of wine and women. He also tended to be somewhat careless. One day, in the course of my duties, I got access to his desk where I discovered a set of officer candidate insignia. I immediately lifted them from his drawer for my own use. Officers had no curfew restrictions, so the insignia could come in handy for nighttime activities, I reasoned. Privately, I hoped that I would be able to use the insignia as part of some sort of disguise someday.

As the months went by, I began to gain increased acceptance within the office. Because of my Japanese ancestry and language fluency, I began to blend into their tasks and they began to see me as one of them. At least it seemed that way. With each added responsibility I gained an extra measure of freedom. I finally reached a major watershed when they entrusted me with maintaining the log for incoming documents. I had lucked into a very valuable source of intelligence information and it was up to me to make the most of the opportunity. I first devised a filing system that impressed the staff. This not only gave me free reign over the documents, but also gave me control over a system that I understood better than anyone else in the office. Access to the documents was also eased by the fact that they were stored in footlockers rather than safes as we used in the U.S. military. Footlockers were used by Japanese forces to facilitate evacuation in any kind of emergency. Luckily for me, the measure was instituted in Manila because the Philippine area was deemed to be in a combat zone.

Once accessibility to the documents was established, my problem was to find some way to get the information to the U.S. side. The colonel issued strict orders that there was to be no outside contact once we entered his quarters. I had to find some way of getting out of his quarters.

One way, I surmised, was to break a house rule, which would not result in criminal prosecution but could lead to being expelled from his quarters. When I first came to live there, he made it clear that I could not invite female guests into my quarters without his permission.

I decided to break that rule to see if I could be expelled from his quarters. One night, during his absence, I went to the home of a Spanish woman who resided two doors away from the colonel. I felt free to approach her because every day, as we returned home in the colonel's car, she would smile and wave at us. I struck up a conversation with her and eventually asked her if she had ever been in the colonel's house. She said she hadn't, but added that she had always been curious to see how a high-ranking Japanese officer lived. So I invited her over and gave her a personal tour of his quarters. Having satisfied her curiosity, she went home right away.

Just as I had predicted, the Taiwanese servants, who were itching for revenge, used the incident to get back at me. The next morning, the colonel's valet reported the incident to him, and I was summoned to his dining room. He dressed me down, saying that I had spoiled his day with the revelation that I had broken an ironclad house rule.

He fixed a withering glare on me and shouted, "You will no longer be allowed to enjoy the hospitality of this house. I want you out of here!" I could just imagine the Taiwanese servants laughing and rejoicing over their coup. Little did they realize that they had played right into my hands.

I tried to appear as contrite as possible as I retreated to my room to pick up my meager possessions. I packed quickly, got into the colonel's car, and that was the last that I saw of the colonel's quarters.

At the office, the colonel instructed a warrant officer who was the chief of the Administrative Division to make arrangements to billet me with the civilian employees. The billet turned out to be the former British Club. Since there were three other civilian employees, I drew Mr. Shimazu, who was conscripted for service in the Philippines as a civil servant. I couldn't have been happier with that arrangement because it allowed me greater freedom of movement after normal duty hours.

In the meantime, the tide of the war began to turn against the Japanese forces in the South Pacific and in Southeast Asia. Their losses mounted. Soon, there was an upsurge in guerrilla activities in the Philippines.

The Kempeitai, with its vast network of sources, began a systematic campaign to apprehend all Filipinos suspected of being either members of or having some form of association with the Filipino guerrilla groups. Those who were rounded up were put through mock trials, sentenced, and then put into Mantinlupa Prison. The trials were highly superficial with only weak attempts made to simulate fairness and this was done only as a sop to jurists on the Japanese side who insisted that true justice be upheld in the courtrooms. Unfortunately, those with moral qualms had little control over the situation actually prevailing in the military courts.

Each trial was presided over by a panel of three judges who listened to charges against the accused. After arguments were presented, a recess would be called and a verdict rendered. In reality, the disposition of each case was predetermined in highly peremptory manner by the colonel. The findings of the courts and the verdicts would be written up and mimeographed even before the conclusion of the trial itself. I was very familiar with the procedure because mimeographing of the procedures and verdicts were tasks assigned to me during the trials.

During my first week of assignment to the judge advocate general's office, while I was undergoing training with the mimeographing machine, I ran some mimeographs off on scrap paper. In the process, I ran across trial papers on myself that had been scrapped with a set of findings and a death verdict that had been printed up even before I had been tried. The discovery had a chilling effect on me. Perhaps I shouldn't have been as stunned as I was, since I was always aware of the consequences of conviction by a military tribunal. But it was a sobering discovery. I shuddered to think of how close I had come to being beheaded. Once more, I was thankful that I didn't succumb to all the torture and confess. I also realized how easy it would be for the Japanese military to reinstate the charges against me. One crank of the mimeograph machine would be all that it would take to bring on my beheading. I was determined to be even more careful about being lulled into complacency by my newly acquired freedom of movement.

The Filipino guerrillas who were sentenced to death were taken to the Chinese cemetery outside of Manila City and decapitated. This was normally performed in groups of ten. I felt helpless knowing that this was going on and able to do nothing.

Occasionally, I was forced to fill in as an interpreter at the trials. About all I could do was to tone down some of the replies of those being accused so that the Japanese wouldn't be so harsh on them.

Day after day I bided my time, waiting for an opportunity to establish some sort of network. Then one day, a Filipino woman came to the judge advocate's office seeking permission to visit her husband, who was confined at the Mantinlupa Prison. She identified herself as the wife of Ernesto Tupas. She said that she had gone to the prison to visit her husband but was refused entry. She was told that she needed the approval of a captain at the judge advocate general's office. All prisoners incarcerated as guerrillas or suspected guerrillas required the permission of the captain for visitation rights.

Tupas was a sergeant with the Philippine Scouts when the war broke out and he was subsequently assigned to G2. He also participated in the Bataan campaign. He was subsequently released from Cabuanatang Prison because he was a Filipino. Tupas later became a member of the ROTC guerrillas, serving as their provost marshal. The ROTC guerrillas were so named because the nucleus of the organization was made up of former ROTC students. Tupas's active involvement with the guerrilla movement was the cause of his return to prison.

I obtained permission for Mrs. Tupas to visit her husband, which she greatly appreciated. I told her that she should come back to see me whenever she wanted to visit him since I was in a position to help her. She impressed me as a gracious woman with a quiet demeanor that cloaked her fierce pride and fervent dedication to her husband. She had every reason to distrust me, but somehow she seemed to understand that I was really trying to help her.

In the meantime, I did some checking on my own. I occasionally visited Mantinlupa Prison in the company of the captain and on one such visit, I learned that Tupas was being employed at the prison power plant because of his skill in the electrical trade.

Fortunately, I was able to see Tupas on one of these visits. I told him where I worked at Japanese Army Headquarters and that I had encouraged his wife to contact me whenever she needed a visitation pass to see him. I told him that as long as I was in that position, I could be of help to them.

The visitation pass was a mimeographed form and all it required was the captain's *han* stamp to authenticate it. The *han* stamp, or *hanko*, as it was called in Japan, is a personal seal that works much like an official stamp, except that unlike ours, it is done in calligraphy and it carries the force of a legal signature. Whenever I was on night duty, I would mimeograph some forms and authenticate them with the captain's stamp, which he left in an unlocked desk drawer. This enabled me to give out passes at will.

I was in serious need of developing some contacts to relay the intelligence I had collected to the American side, and the Filipino guerrilla force struck me as a possible conduit.

I also examined other alternatives. One weekend, on a chance, I visited a Filipino colonel who headed the intelligence unit of the Philippine Constabulary. I had known him before the Japanese takeover and he greeted me heartily. But the minute I mentioned the guerrillas to him, he backed off. That set off alarm bells in my head because he could very well turn me in to the Kempeitai. Suddenly, I felt very vulnerable and I backed away too. I politely excused myself and left his office. I was not about to risk getting caught again in the web of the Kempeitai.

One of the great challenges of undercover work lies in determining the credibility of sources. Under desperate circumstances, it is easy to succumb to false signals. And yet, at times, one is never sure whether to be guided by optimism or pessimism. It comes down to

153

weighing facts and instincts. One such incident occurred about a month after my aborted contact with the Filipino colonel.

I was approached by Horatio Consing, the son-in-law of a Filipino family that I had befriended during the war. He said that there was a Father Monahan who was eager to meet me to arrange for my escape from the Philippines. My heart leaped when I heard the proposal but after the incident with the Filipino colonel, I had to wonder whether this was a trap being set for me by the Kempeitai. I asked him who Father Monahan was, what did he really want from me, why was he doing this, when was the escape to take place, and where was I to be sent? All he told me was that while walking around town, he was approached by an unidentified individual who requested that Father Monahan's wishes be conveyed very discreetly to me. I suspected that Horatio was involved in guerrilla activities and that Father Monahan was a pseudonym but I couldn't be sure so I told Horatio that I would reply only to Father Monahan himself. I told him that I could go anywhere for a meeting after dark just as long as I had sufficient time to make my own arrangements to get away from my quarters. I waited for a reply with hope and trepidation but no word came.

Three months later, I learned that Horatio had been apprehended by the Kempeitai and sentenced to death. I was sickened by the news because he was such a fine young man belonging to a respectable Filipino family. I also had a strong hunch that he was a bonafide contact. In his book, *Spy Catchers in the U.S. Army in the War with Japan*, Duval Edwards writes that at that time, a Filipino guerrilla unit led by an American and referred to as Anderson's Guerrillas had in fact been trying to get me out, at the direction of MacArthur's headquarters.

It had become clear that there was no point in trying to develop a reliable contact using conventional approaches. An alternative was to stage a breakout from Mantinlupa Prison to free as many guerrillas as possible. I met with Tupas to feel him out on the plan. Tupas leaped at the proposal.

Our strategy was to first alert members of his guerrilla organization to the plan. In the meantime, Mrs. Tupas would serve as a courier between myself and her husband. She was to use the mimeographed passes that I had provided her to get in and out of prison. I added an authorization to her visitation pass that allowed her to bring food parcels into the prison compound for her husband. Concealed in the prepared food parcels or baskets brought into the prison were tools that were needed for the breakout. The bravery displayed by Mrs. Tupas in performing her role was truly inspiring. It reinforced my own determination to see the mission through to the end.

Through surveillance missions coordinated with the guerrillas operating outside of the prison compound, we learned about the security measures regularly observed by the Japanese prison garrison. The officer of the day, accompanied by a squad of Japanese soldiers, conducted one nightly check, which took place just before midnight. This was done almost every night.

The next step was to obtain some Japanese Army uniforms. I requested four sets of regular soldier's uniforms and one officer's uniform from the ROTC guerrillas, who were conducting constant raids against Japanese units. We hid them at a strategic site so we could change into them very quickly.

We scheduled the breakout in August 1944. At a designated time and place, I met four Filipino guerrillas and had them change into the Japanese soldier's uniforms. I dressed in the officer's uniform to impersonate the officer of the day. Before starting off, I pinned on the officer candidate's insignia, which I had stolen months before, to make my uniform complete.

Just before midnight, we moved silently toward the prison gate. We were blessed that night because there was no inspection by the duty officer. We began marching to the gate. As soon as the guard spotted the red sash of the officer of the day, which I was wearing, he and the other guards bowed deeply. Without a word, we disarmed the guards who were taken completely by surprise. Within five minutes we had the prison office under our control. This allowed the other guerrillas who were in hiding outside the gates to rush in and secure the prison armory.

Simultaneously, Tupas, who positioned himself in the power plant, short-circuited the entire prison electrical network. All of the ROTC guerrillas and anyone else wishing to be freed were released from their cells. Within half an hour we were able to clear out of the prison. I immediately returned to my billet in Manila while the liberated prisoners raced toward Mount Rizal.

Next morning, the director of the prison came to the colonel's office to report the breakout. With animated gestures accompanying each explanation, the prison director reported the details of the breakout and I watched the colonel's face turn from impassiveness to a look of shock and incredulity. The director was severely reprimanded, especially for allowing the armory to be ransacked. According to the director, the chief guard on duty at the armory pleaded with the guerrillas to leave some of the weapons to quell any uprisings by the hardened criminals and political prisoners still left behind but all they left him was a shotgun and one round of ammunition. The rest was taken by the guerrillas. With that the colonel went into a rage. I tried to make a good show of being troubled over the incident with the rest of the office staff.

Thereafter, I was able to send out all the intelligence that I wanted to through Tupas and his group. The guerrillas had contacts with groups who would then deliver the information to U.S. forces by telegraph. The information we sent was predominantly combat intelligence.

The modus operandi revolved around secret drop sites and clandestine meeting places developed by Tupas and his men. The primary meeting place was the Ayala Bridge where I would meet Tupas or a designated courier around 11:30 P.M. Tupas would have a *bunka*, or rowboat, ready and we would get in and drift on the Pasay River pretending to be torch fishing.

Our secondary meeting place was the parking lot at Quiapo Church. On those occasions, Tupas drove a delivery truck that resembled the ones making deliveries to the Quiapo Market. To avoid suspicion we drove only along the main highways and Tupas invariably provided me with native clothes to wear while we were together.

We allowed ourselves thirty minutes leeway to make it to any meeting. Any wait beyond thirty minutes meant scrubbing that particular contact. The standing agreement was that we would then meet the following evening but two hours later than the usual time to avoid surveillance. After each meeting, we would decide on when or where the next meeting would take place. There was never any information passed in writing; everything was by word of mouth to avoid incriminating evidence. I was also given a phone number to call if I had anything urgent to pass on. For such calls, the code message was "Borja to Ernesto," and it meant that the meeting was to take place at the Jai Alai Building between 10:30 P.M. and 11:30 P.M. that very day.

The Japanese Signal Corps was monitoring the airwaves and soon began attempts to locate the source of the Filipino transmissions. For that reason, the guerrilla groups were unable to transmit more than once from the same site. They were constantly on the run and transmitting from various areas. I had no confirmation that my information ever successfully reached the American forces. I didn't mind if the Filipinos took credit for the flow of intelligence as long as it helped the U.S. forces that were moving toward the Philippines by then.

A few years ago, I was gratified to read the following account in a U.S. Army publication:

> With his new network, Sakakida was able to begin sending regular intelligence reports mainly dealing with shipping information and the movement of Japanese troops. Perhaps the most important of the reports concerned the assembly of a Japanese force at Davao in the Southern Philippine Island of Mindanao. Approximately 15 Japanese troop transports and destroyers were believed to have headed south for the front lines.

According to an account in the book by Edward Drea entitled *MacArthur's ULTRA: Codebreaking and the War against Japan, 1942–1945*, the codebreakers reported the departure of the *Take* (pronounced Tah-kay) convoy from Manila to Davao. It confirmed my report from Manila about the impending landing of a huge Japanese force. Forewarned, American submarines lay in wait for the convoy comprising nine transports and seven escorts, carrying well over 13,000 troops. Within ten minutes, three transports were sunk and 1,290 troops aboard them perished. About 6,800 soldiers were rescued from the sea by escort vessels but all of their ordinance and supplies were lost. The result was a debacle for the Japanese.

What happened thereafter at a damage assessment meeting held by the Japanese command was fortuitous. They believed their codes to be secure. According to Drea's account, the Japanese command speculated that sudden bursts of radio traffic, indicating the movement of a large convoy may have tipped the Americans off at that time compromising the need-to-know rule or there was the possibility that spies working the Manila Harbor may have been the source of the leak. That assessment resulted in the old codes being retained by the Japanese command, allowing ULTRA to continue the successful decoding of Japanese messages without interruption.

Drea adds that

> Southwest Pacific Headquarters actually did have a spy working as a handyman inside the Japanese Judge Advocate General's Office in Manila. . . . The resourceful sergeant had reported the departure of the *Take* convoy, so the Japanese had some basis for their almost paranoid concern for spies, which deflected their attention from the possibility of compromised codes.

Actually, one of my main sources for the *Take* operation was a judge advocate officer who was picked to accompany the convoy. I even helped him pack for the mission.

A month after the first prison break, I was approached by Tupas and members of another group to stage a second prison break. I was reluctant on two counts. First, it had only been a month since the last breakout and the wariness of the prison officials was still high. Second, the security system in effect at the prison since the previous breakout had to be studied thoroughly lest we put ourselves in the position of courting disaster on the next try. As it turned out, there were no new security measures instituted at the prison after the first breakout and only a minimum number of weapons had been brought into the armory as replacements.

I was wary about the second raid but nevertheless, six weeks after the first raid, they mounted a similar operation without me. The plan was not quite the same and was staged in the wee hours of the morning.

This time the director of prisons was fired and the Mantinlupa Prison was reorganized. Overall control of prison activities was turned over to the Philippine Constabulary and the constabulary itself was reorganized under the guidance of the Japanese military.

Colonel Sisson was appointed the commandant of Mantinlupa Prison in the aftermath of the incident. He immediately instituted strict military controls over prison procedures. Prison visitations by family members were double-checked by prison guards who were required to contact the judge advocate's office as a matter of procedure to verify the authenticity of the passes issued under the captain's signature.

On one of my visits to Mantinlupa, I had an opportunity to speak to Colonel Sisson. I asked him if he could adopt a more lenient visitation policy for family members since the main Japanese units were located about fifty miles north of the prison and he was not under close observation. His reply was curt and right to the point. He saw no need to accord them any added visitation privileges.

I understood him clearly and I did not approach him with further entreaties, lest I be suspected of sympathizing with someone in prison. In hindsight, I shudder to think what could have happened had I persisted in pushing for further reforms in prison procedures. It could very well have led to my undoing just as conditions were changing in my favor. Had I come under renewed suspicion by the Kempeitai, I am certain that some of the their personnel would have delighted in working me over again. That could have been fatal for me.

Besides, by then, there was no call for hasty action. All of the important Filipino guerrillas had been freed and the colonel's new security measures were no longer of any real concern to me. In addition, it was increasingly evident that the tide of the war in the Pacific was shifting in favor of the Allies.

By October 1944, Allied forces under the command of General MacArthur had already established a firm foothold on Leyte Island. The most telling proof of the U.S. presence came in the form of air raids conducted by U.S. aircraft on military targets in and around Manila. The intensity of the air raids increased with each passing day. For me, each air raid was a morale booster. As long as I stayed

159

out of harm's way and avoided any gaffes, there was hope of surviving the war. As the air raids escalated, the Japanese 14th Army Headquarters was compelled to move from the Finance Building in Manila to Fort McKinley. The judge advocate's office took over the office space in the former U.S. Military Canteen Building.

The advantage offered by Fort McKinley was that it had air raid bunkers. As I listened to the bombs exploding around us, I recalled the joke that I had shared on Corregidor with Colonel Wood about bombs being rained down on me by my ancestors for translating Japanese documents for the American side. Back then, we both laughed as we sat in a shower stall to protect ourselves. I chuckled to myself as I recalled the incident but this time, the thought also occurred to me that was I getting dumped on no matter which way the war shifted. Somehow, that made me laugh too. However, I quickly caught myself. I didn't want the others to think that I was enjoying the bombing. Actually, in a perverse sort of way, I was enjoying it.

Chapter 11

BAGUIO: ESCAPE AND FREEDOM

The island-hopping strategy pursued by the Allied forces in the South Pacific theater of war brought the Philippines back into the zone of active combat by the fall of 1944. Even more ominous to the Japanese military command was the realization that the war was headed toward Japan itself.

The events confirmed the worst fears of some of Japan's best military minds. Men such as Adm. Isoroku Yamamoto, who plotted the attack on Pearl Harbor, and Gen. Tomoyuki Yamashita, who stunned the defenders of Malaya and Singapore with a series of brilliant and daring diversionary tactics, believed that short of a quick victory, a small, resource-poor Japan would ultimately be no match for a great, resource-rich and industrially powerful America. The Japanese navy, in particular, produced a cadre of well-traveled officers who were opposed to a long drawn-out war with the West. However, like all good soldiers, once war was declared, they willingly and loyally committed themselves to the war effort. There are historians who contend that the bane of Japan and the Japanese diplomatic and military policy-making process was the ultranationalism that dominated the Japanese domestic political scene during that era.

161

In the climate of militarism that reigned during the 1930s, ideological probity and political correctness took precedence over enlightened political and military strategy. In what has come to be referred to as "government by assassination," the liberal wing of Japanese politics, which opposed rampant militarism, was virtually wiped out by radical Japanese military officers and their political supporters. The more far-seeing and prudent military officers were isolated and deprived of a political constituency that could have carried the nation in another direction—away from war with the United States and the West. For officers who were in that wing of the military—Admiral Yamamoto, Generals Yamashita and Homma, General Iida, who sealed off the Burma Road, and General Imamura, whose forces captured the Dutch East Indies—battlefield feats did little to enhance their political influence. Instead, they became targets of internal jealousy and partisan politics. Incredibly, both General Homma, who led the victorious campaign in the Philippines, and General Yamashita, who was victorious in Malaya and Singapore, were summarily relieved of their commands at the height of their careers. Homma returned to an assignment in Japan and Yamashita was sent to the Manchurian front. General Yamashita, who was then regarded as one of Japan's great heroes, was not even allowed a stopover in Japan to visit with his family. The possibility that he might gain an audience with the emperor during a home visit and that he represented moderate views was not acceptable to radical politicians and the right wing of the military, which controlled the cabinet of General Hideki Tojo. Politically, it was a time of nationalism turning xenophobic, and unfortunately for men like Yamashita, it was controlled by the military high command. Yamashita languished without complaint in Manchuria during the most fierce fighting in the South Pacific.

The political downfall of the Tojo cabinet finally brought Yamashita back to the Pacific. However, by then, the battle of the Philippines was all but lost for Japan. John Deane Potter, in his book *The Life and Death of a Japanese General,* states that General Yamashita replaced General Kuroda, who was criticized for, among other things, "devoting too much time to golf, reading, and personal matters."

Yamashita was not unaware of the situation in Asia. By all accounts, he was a man who kept his feelings to himself and he watched with grave concern as the island of Saipan fell to American forces. In his view, the fall of Saipan was a crucial American victory because it put the Japanese homeland within striking range of American long-range bombers. At the same time, the Japanese advance toward India was being stymied by British forces along the border of Burma, and for the first time since their stunning string of victories in the Asian and Pacific theaters of war, the Japanese high command faced the possibility of defeat on every front.

Within days of the defeat at Saipan, the Tojo cabinet fell and was replaced by a cabinet formed by Kuniaki Koiso. Only then was Yamashita summoned to Tokyo. Many of Japan's top generals objected to the assignment of Yamashita to a rapidly crumbling battlefront in the Philippines. But he was asked to take the post and he did.

The arrival of General Yamashita in Manila had no relevance to me personally. I did get a glimpse of him when he arrived because he initially set up his headquarters at Fort McKinley where I was located.

General Yamashita's stint in Manila and at Fort McKinley was short-lived. As the military situation worsened, he saw no point in including Manila in his battle plan. Manila had a fine harbor and airfield but beyond that, there were definite liabilities. The problem of feeding the huge population was prohibitive, the major buildings of the city were highly flammable, and the flat terrain would require far more troops for its defense than he could afford under the circumstances. From a strategic standpoint, it was a view shared by General MacArthur when he himself ordered the evacuation of Manila.

Yamashita decided to move his headquarters to Baguio, the former summer capital, located about five thousand feet up in the mountains of northern Luzon. He left only a small force in Manila to protect the evacuation of troops and supplies and to destroy the main bridges, railways, and highways leading into the city to slow

163

the relentless American advance. Yamashita's plan was to block all of the mountain passes to Baguio in an attempt to delay action.

His plan was destined to fail. Unfortunately, Yamashita was dogged by interservice rivalry. Both the 4th Air Force, commanded by Lieutenant General Tominaga, a supporter of General Tojo, and the naval units stationed in Manila resented the retreat ordered by Yamashita. The naval commander, Vice Admiral Okochi, insisted on taking his orders from naval headquarters in Tokyo. Unbeknownst to Yamashita, Okochi decided to ignore the order to retreat and set up his own defense of Manila relying on sailors who had never been trained in ground combat. The men fought bravely knowing that there was no chance of survival. It was under those circumstances that many of those men went berserk, killing innocent Filipinos and raping the women who had the misfortune to be left in Manila. The rape of Manila was a sad chapter that Yamashita was to pay for during the war crimes trials even though it was caused by rebellious commanders.

All of the turmoil and anguish caused by these incidents forced the Japanese to turn away from concern for prisoners like myself. I bided my time, looking for an opportunity to get away, and realizing that if I didn't do it then, I would have to go along with the retreating Japanese units. Also, I sensed that as the retreat accelerated, resentment against me mounted. I became a convenient target for the frustrations of those around me.

During the first phase of the withdrawal from Fort McKinley, General Yamashita moved his forward headquarters to Ipo Dam. In the interim, attempts to blockade all mountain passages to Baguio went ahead as planned to blunt the American offensive. Within four months, however, the relentless American advance forced him to withdraw all the way to Baguio.

My immediate fate was still tied to the judge advocate's staff. Our own withdrawal to Baguio was orderly. We rode north on trucks and the trip was without incident. In the retreat to Baguio, the colonel lost his Taiwanese cook, servant, and driver. All three were assigned to the 14th Army Labor Battalion which was organized to clear new paths of retreat into the mountain areas. I was fortunate to avoid being part of the contingency measures involving forced labor. Instead, I was picked to fill the void left by the departure of the three men. My responsibility was to look after the colonel's personal needs. But in reality, I ended up looking after his entire staff.

Baguio was the original site of the Philippine Military Academy, which was patterned after West Point. It was also where the Command and Staff School of the Philippines was situated. Prior to the outbreak of the war, it was used to train American colonels and senior Philippine officers who were being groomed to command the Philippine Army divisions. I found it very impressive.

Baguio was a town with modern facilities and amenities befitting the summer capital of the Philippine Commonwealth. It had the look, grace, and charm of a capital center with broad well-kept streets and architecturally pleasing government buildings that did not have the severely functional look of buildings built strictly for administrative use. The town was wisely built in a cool and lush mountain setting, away from the sweltering heat that pervaded Manila in the summer. There were no high-rise buildings or bothersome traffic or noise, which gave the township a look of order and settled refinement. I could tell that in peacetime, it was a place that bustled with restaurants, boutiques, and a fetching market place for which it was noted. The climate at Baguio reminded me a great deal of the mountainous Haleakala peak on the island of Maui in Hawaii. In January, when we got there it was cool during the day and quite chilly at night, forcing all of us to use blankets.

General Yamashita's headquarters was set up in the Baguio Hospital Building. The judge advocate's office was also located there. It struck me as curious that even as operations began, no attempt was made to remove the Red Cross sign from the building.

Living quarters for the judge advocate's staff were set up in a nearby church. Since the colonel's household staff was gone, it fell upon me to do the cooking. It wasn't a bad assignment. I could have done much worse. I had never been trained as a cook but they had no choice but to eat whatever I prepared. And in time of war, there were not likely to be complaints about the food as long as hunger was regularly kept at bay. There were some benefits to be accrued from the assignment. As a staff officer of the 14th Army, the colonel received a daily allotment of rations that included rice, other staples, and even candy and liquor. Others, even within his own department, were forced to live off of the land. I felt fortunate in being spared from foraging and scrounging around in town or the surrounding jungle for food. As I gained control of the rations, I was able to stash away such nonperishables as uncooked rice to take with me if I succeeded in escaping.

Again I was mindful of avoiding suspicion. I figured that the more I blended in with the people and their everyday activities, the better my chances would be for escape.

As the events of the war began to favor the United States, the colonel's disposition became worse. He continued to be overbearing and arrogant, but his outbreaks of temper increased. Every military setback and every bureaucratic snafu set him off. He had a tendency to vent his spleen on anyone in his line of fire. My dislike of him was exacerbated by anxieties of my own, however. I didn't mind authority in a military setting, but I was getting tired of being stepped on and I was also getting edgy about finding some way to escape.

Meanwhile, as the Japanese Army units moved out of Manila at General Yamashita's orders, the naval units moved in on the pretext of destroying all naval installations in the city. What followed was described by John Deane Potter as "one of the most savage conflicts of the war, more bitter and barbaric than the seige of Stalingrad." As conditions worsened, Yamashita proposed returning all prisoners to the Americans for logistical reasons, but he was rebuffed by the navy and air force.

To me, the news was good and bad. Good because people like me were becoming extraneous to their immediate military needs and bad because people like the colonel were reluctant to let us go. I knew that I was useful as a houseboy but I had no desire to become a human shield. If I were to die, I still intended to die for the American side.

I finally decided that it was time to make a break. The one thing that I didn't want to chance was being caught in a cross fire because of my Japanese face. There were many Japanese soldiers who would have had no compunction about shooting me under desperate conditions, and the American soldiers would certainly have seen me as a Japanese in no-man's-land.

166

It was not long before an opportunity to escape presented itself. When the defense of Baguio became untenable, preparations began for a retreat into the mountains. I had contracted malaria in Bataan and also had developed beriberi. Due to my afflictions, I asked the colonel for permission to spend some time recuperating before moving again. I was actually not feeling well and that helped me to convince the colonel and the staff that I was really too ill to travel just then. As the days passed, I made it look like my condition was worsening. When the order was finally issued to leave, I informed the colonel that it would be best for them to go ahead without me. I told them that I was just a handyman and that I would probably be of no use to them in combat. I added that I would only be an extra mouth to feed and being sick, I would slow down their retreat.

By then, the colonel was too preoccupied with operational matters to give me much thought. He turned to me and with the contemptuous look that was so characteristic of him, he said, "All right, you can rest and recuperate here for a few days. But as soon as you feel better, you are to rejoin us. Is that clear?"

"Yes sir," I replied weakly and I made a half-hearted attempt to arise from my reclining position but before I could even brace myself to do so, he had swung around and was gone. I was overjoyed.

After the caravan that they joined was out of sight, I quickly got up to prepare for my own departure. First I gathered up all the food that I had hidden away. I thought of sergeant Nolan who had stashed away rations on Corregidor and it made me laugh as I remembered what happened back then. "Good man; lots of common sense," I said to myself.

The most precious thing that I had stored was small pouches of rice that I could take along and cook. I also packed parts of a Japanese mess kit to cook and eat with and also a knife that I had squirreled away in the kitchen. The last item I pulled out was a pistol that I had stolen from the office along with some ammunition. As pistols go, it was a huge piece, something on the order of a .357 magnum. I would have preferred something smaller to conceal among my possessions but "beggars can't be choosers," I said to myself.

I decided not to leave immediately because nightfall was nearing

167

and I knew it would be cold up there in the highlands. Besides, there was always the danger of running into stragglers trying to catch up with the retreating Japanese units. So I gathered up whatever remained in the kitchen and prepared myself a meal. By ordinary standards, it wasn't much of a meal but I savored the privacy in which I was able to dine for a change. I was even able to enjoy some tea with a cigarette. By then, a noticeable chill had set in, so I wrapped myself up in a blanket to try to get a good night's sleep.

It felt strange to be alone and unfettered by captivity. For the first time in about three years, I was free of shackles. As darkness fell, an eerie silence settled over the church and its surroundings. I began to reflect upon the beauty and serenity of Baguio. It was dark but I could see the surrounding woods through the window. Up above, the sky was clear and the moon and stars glittered as if to draw attention to the galaxy. It was a shame that there was so little time to enjoy something that was so natural and basic to our existence. Soon the fighting would begin again to bring more death and destruction to this quiet little place in the mountains, I thought. I fell into a deep sleep.

In the morning, I got up with a start. Rays of sunshine were already streaming through the window above me and for a brief moment I felt disoriented. Unlike other mornings, it was quiet and there was no one around. My oversensitive instincts made me fear that I had been discovered and was being watched. I jumped out of bed and looked around but I could see no one. I felt good again and I could feel my adrenaline beginning to flow. I quickly washed, ate a few morsels of food, and checked my supplies. I then surveyed the area from the vantage point of the church tower and saw no movement or sign of a Japanese military presence so I set off into the surrounding woods.

Most of the first day I wandered aimlessly through the jungle. My goal was to find the American lines but I had no compass and the jungle has a way of disorienting one at every new turn.

I spent a few days living on rations plus fruits and edible grass that I foraged in the jungle. Knowledge of plants from my days in Hawaii greatly abetted my survival. The going was relatively easy during the day because the climate was mildly warm in the mountains but it was uncomfortably cold at night. I wrapped my blanket about me, and even though I was probably secure in the jungle, sleep was always light. It is the lot of a POW to feel insecure even in relatively secure places.

There is something about a jungle that can be forbidding and yet intimate. One is never familiar with jungle ecology until one enters and confronts it. Trees, bushes, vines, plants of every kind and description, fallen leaves and the climate in which they thrive all combine to produce a tangled web that is resistant to attempts at forcible entry or passage. The animals around me understood the law of the jungle instinctively. They moved around with ease, as if to humble me in their habitat. But I welcomed the presence of birds and animals and like them, I eventually learned not to challenge the jungle unwisely. There is a limit to how much one can cut through even with the sharpest machete. If I moved, it was only in terms of what the landscape and environment allowed me. But what this adjustment brings is a certain sense—a sense of the jungle that can be gauged only in terms of the sights, smells, and sounds that it emits in its own inimitable way.

It was after days of getting acclimated that I reached a distinct break in the jungle. As I came upon a clearing, I could sense a human presence close by. My instincts immediately signalled caution. I pushed on out of a mixture of curiousity and desperation. That was how I came upon a village of Igorots.

Over the centuries, isolated tribal communities with unique identities had emerged in the lush uplands of the Philippines. One of these tribes was the Igorots. In the Tagalog dialect, Igorot means mountaineer. At one time, the word carried pejorative connotations, none the least of which was a reputation for being headhunters.

One distinguishing feature of the Igorots was their short physical stature and the diminutive look that pervaded everything in their village including the thatched huts that they lived in. I approached the village with some trepidation. I had narrowly avoided a beheading at the hands of the Japanese military and I wondered if my luck would continue to hold. But there was no turning back or easy way around the settlement. After all, the jungle was their natural habitat

169

and buffer against outsiders and they knew their way around the uplands much better than I did.

As a cluster of villagers approached me, I tried to look as friendly and as amiable as possible in spite of my bedraggled appearance. To my enormous relief, I was greeted cordially and with a spontaneity that was both disarming and heartwarming. Life as a POW had made me edgy and suspicious of everyone and I was an easy mark for some sign of genuine goodwill.

I didn't speak their language and they didn't speak mine, so we communicated in sign language. For all I know, they may have thought that I was a Japanese soldier. But that didn't matter. What mattered was that I was safe in their midst.

I was shown to an individual hut, which I had to crawl into, and was told through sign language that I would be given something to eat later on. To my astonishment and for whatever reason, that night I was invited to a dog feast sponsored by the chief of the village.

Dog feasts are held only on special occasions by the Igorots. For the feast, a dog is kept on the verge of starvation until the very day of the feast. The dog is then fed huge amounts of boiled rice. The dog eats ravenously until it is bloated. At this point, tribe members begin dancing around the dog beating it with sticks. This causes the dog to die of internal hemorrhaging. They then cut the dog open and the warm, blood-soaked rice is served to the chief and on down the tribal pecking order. The dog is then pit-roasted. To say that I was taken aback by it all was a gross understatement, but protocol and etiquette demanded that I join in so I did. Besides, I had a good reason not to get on the wrong side of these people. I ate as little as the occasion would permit. All the while, I tried to praise what they obviously regarded as a delicacy and thanked them again and again for their generosity. After all, they were providing me with food and shelter and their hospitality was genuine.

The rice produced by the Igorots in the lush uplands was outstanding. The rice-based diet that they provided during my stay there allowed me to get over some of my ailments. I stayed there almost a month before deciding that it was time to move on. I thanked my hosts as best as I could and as an Asian, felt bad that there was nothing I could give them in gratitude as was customary.

170

At first glance, the Igorots seemed primitive by Western standards. But during my stay, I learned to appreciate the logic of their ways. Both men and women wore only loin cloths that were not only well suited to their jungle habitat but also to their own hygienic needs. They hunted, tilled the land, and lived in ways that enhanced nature rather than doing violence to it.

Japanese military incursions into Igorot territory were met with armed resistance. It was reported that in jungle fighting, the Japanese forces fared badly against the Igorots, prompting them to bring in some Takasago aborigines from Taiwan to assist in pacifying the Igorots. The level of violence and wanton brutality of the Takasago mercenaries appalled even the Japanese, causing them to call off the experiment.

Very soon, I came upon the first tangible evidence of an American military presence in the Philippines. I got caught in an artillary duel between U.S. forces moving north and Japanese forces moving into the mountains. I was in a kind of no-man's land, but I felt reassured by the presence of American forces not too far away.

As I pushed on, I came upon an area abandoned by the retreating Japanese. To my great delight, I had stumbled upon remnants of a Japanese quartermaster field depot. I found sack after sack of unpolished rice, powdered soy sauce, and other items common to Japanese combat rations.

Not having had a decent meal in weeks since leaving the Igorots, I prepared myself a mess kit full of rice with accompaniments and thoroughly enjoyed dinner. It was then that I made a nearly fatal mistake. It was already dusk and I thought the perfect end to the meal would be a good smoke. I got some tobacco leaves and fashioned them into a roll, then lit it and sat back to savor the moment. Unfortunately, a Japanese artillery observer was on the lookout and saw smoke rising from the spot. Suddenly, I was besieged by an artillery barrage that scared the wits out of me. It had been so quiet and peaceful until then.

I figured I would be safer half way up the mountain so I began moving to a higher spot. As I approached my destination, three shells exploded around me. I was knocked unconscious. Sometime later, when I regained consciousness, I felt a wetness in the area of my abdomen. I felt terrified and helpless. I was bleeding and unable to move. It was pitch dark by then and I had not choice but to lay there until dawn.

At sunup, I examined myself and discovered that I had been hit in the stomach by shrapnel. Not being able to walk, I half-crawled and rolled down the mountainside. Fortunately, there was a little stream several hundred yards from where I had been hit. It took a good portion of the day, but I got there and was able to wash and cleanse my wound. With no medication, I simply washed the wounds every day with water scooped up from the stream.

Three days later, the pain from the infection and the stench that it produced became virtually unbearable. While washing out the wounds, I spotted a piece of shrapnel still embedded in the flesh of my abdomen. As long as the shrapnel was there, there was no way that the wounds would heal. There was also the threat of gangrene setting in. So using a razor blade that I had been carrying, I managed to remove the shrapnel. The pain was almost unbearable, but the flow of blood freed the wounds of much of the pus that had formed around them. I have heard it said that in dire circumstances human beings are sometimes capable of doing amazing things. I was amazed at what I was able to do. Each cut and each jerk required to pull the shrapnel out drove me close to unconsciousness, but fortunately, I was able to get it out. That in itself was like a narcotic; a kind of emotional high that got me through the pain and trauma of it all. To this day, I am grateful that I was given the will to do what I did. Lacking medication, I gathered some fresh weeds growing around the stream and mashed them into a paste to put on the wounds, a treatment I'd learned in Hawaii, and miraculously, it worked. Someone up there must have been looking out for me.

I was unable to move from that spot but the stream saved me. I could at least wash in it and drink from it.

Lying there gazing into the water day after day, I eventually noticed the presence of river crabs. They measured approximately one to one-and-a-half inches in size and every day, I managed to catch three to four of them to have for my dinner. Although they were hardly sufficient to satisfy my hunger, they at least kept me alive. Later on, as I crawled upstream, I came upon a decomposed corpse of a Japanese soldier lying in the stream not too far from where I had been. It was already in a state of decay and full of worms. It was a gruesome sight and the stench was even worse. To think, I was drinking the water from that stream every day! It made me want to retch, but I was too weak to even do that.

About three weeks later, the infections seemed to subside even though there were still gaping holes where scar tissue was struggling to form. I decided to try and move on. I had lost all sense of direction and had no idea where I was headed. For the moment and in my condition, I had to trust fate and my trust turned out to be well founded.

Out of nowhere, a water buffalo appeared. It was the kind of beast of burden that was ridden for transportation and employed to do farm chores in the Philippine countryside for centuries. In no time, the water buffalo became my mode of conveyance. It was a slow-moving creature but docile so that I was able to mount it with little trouble at all. It was a godsend because in my condition, I could never have covered the miles that I did on its strong back.

At this point I began to lose track of time. I had no idea what day it was. Worst of all, I was lost. Travel by water buffalo allowed my wounds to improve markedly. Meanwhile, I kept washing my wounds regularly and applying Mother Nature's poultices to heal them. When I was a child, I used to watch the samurais in Japanese movies doing the same kind of thing with their wounds. I used to have a hard time believing in the effectiveness of folk medicine but there I was, acting out my own struggle for survival. To this day, I feel indebted to nature's gifts to the healing arts.

The water buffalo was slow and had a look of despair and aimlessness, something I didn't need as I started to feel better. As my pain subsided and my mobility increased, I became even more anxious to get to the American lines. I had to hurry and the buffalo was obviously in no hurry to get anywhere. Besides, I was starving. One day, I took out the pistol that I had stolen from the judge advocate's office and shot him.

I skinned the creature and roasted as much of the meat as I thought I could consume on a spit that I rigged over a makeshift fireplace. I felt safe in lighting a fire because there had been abso-

173

lutely no sign or sound of military activity anywhere for a long time. I spent the next four days attempting to dry as much of the meat as I could but that was a total failure. I lacked the salt and other preservatives that were needed to complete the task. Instead, I lost everything as the meat began rotting very quickly. It was a cruel fate for my traveling companion but I was rejuvenated by the meat that I was able to consume.

The only other meat I ate after that came from a couple of field rats. One of the things that I guarded preciously was my unhulled rice. At one of my stops, I placed the bags on a stone ledge, away from the elements. One morning, I got up to find that one of the bags had a gaping hole and much of the contents was gone. I was infuriated even in my condition and I vowed to catch the culprit. I perched a rock above the ledge and then propped it up with two pieces of wood fashioned from fallen branches. I tied strings to the wood so that the rock would fall on the thief when I pulled the strings. For bait, I used the few grains of rice that I had left. The trap worked perfectly. I caught my rat, skinned it, and roasted it over a fire. While the thought of eating rat meat may have seemed revolting at one time, I had to admit that it tasted very good.

After that, I decided that I would follow the Asing River wherever it would take me. But my health deteriorated. Malaria, beriberi, and dysentery, all familiar afflictions, began to get the best of me. I became so weak that all I could muster was a few steps before taking a rest.

My walking hours took on a kind of pattern. Early in the morning, I would try to walk as far as my fever-wracked body would take me. By early afternoon, I would be overcome by high fever and then chills that would send me into convulsions until late into the night. By this time, my clothes were absolutely filthy and my nightly bouts with dysentery would force me to go into the stream to clean myself off in the morning. The water was invariably cold, which made me tremble even more. But there was no alternative, I had to do it.

I had also become infested with body lice. At least once a day, I would take off my clothing and run my hands down the seams to squash the white lice between my forefinger and thumb. Crushing

174

the insects would coat my clothing with red blood—my own blood that the lice had been feeding on all night.

I felt so weak that for the first time I began to have doubts about my survival. I was not ready to give up, not after having come that far. Nevertheless, I was near starvation again and I was verging on delirium. The fever had begun to make inroads on my mental faculties.

Then it happened—just like a miracle. I could sense movement and hear voices headed in my direction. I quickly hid from view. As weak and listless as I was, I was suddenly charged with excitement. I marveled at what the flow of adrenaline could do even to a very sick person. Peering out from my hiding place, I saw about six men in full combat gear coming toward me. Then I could hear them speaking English. It was music to my ears. Yet, I had doubts. They wore helmets that reminded me of the German Army and they wore uniforms and chevrons that were unfamiliar. As they drew close, I saw that their gun belts and canteens were like those we used to carry and they had "U.S." inscribed on them. More conclusively, I was sure I heared American slang being spoken. They were American GIs and not German reinforcements sent to aid the Japanese. I stepped out of my hiding place and approached them warily. Since I looked Japanese, I was afraid they would shoot first and ask questions later. I shouted, "Don't shoot, I'm an American."

They seemed startled, and I must have been a sight—filthy, emaciated, disheveled—lurching out of the jungle and speaking American English. At first, they didn't seem to know what to make of me. I could understand that. So I repeated that I was an American.

They came to me and began looking me over very carefully. They said they were members of the 37th Infantry Regiment on a sweep of the area to locate stragglers from Japanese units.

"Stragglers?" I asked. "You mean the Japanese are on the run?"

They looked at me quizzically. Finally, one of them asked, "You mean you don't know that the war's over?" I was momentarily stupefied. I could hardly believe what I had just heard. "No," I replied. "The war ended in August," he continued. "What month is it now?" I asked in a somewhat embarassed tone. "It's September 1945," he replied. I was shocked. I had been wandering around since April,

175

delirious from hunger, illness, and my wounds and I had lost all track of time. Thoughts began to dance around in my head— gyrating thoughts that had been suppressed and held there devoid of emotion for fear that I would lose control of myself. I was free and I had forgotten what it was like to think and feel like everybody else. I felt good but at that juncture, even feeling good had to be tentative. One of the soldiers finally broke the spell by offering me cigarettes and chewing gum. They had no food to give me.

They told me to follow the path that they had taken and I would find their unit. I thanked them and started back. The first thing that I did was to tear open a stick of gum. I stuck it in my mouth and chewed furiously, letting the taste dissolve soothingly into my parched taste buds. As long as I live, I'll never forget that taste!

As hard as I tried, it took me another day and a half to make it to the infantry regiment camp. As I neared the encampment, a sentry stopped me.

What followed was totally unexpected. He demanded all of my personal belongings. I thought this was part of a security procedure but as it turned out, he was looking for things to keep for himself. He pointed to his wrist and kept saying, *"tokei, tokei."* The word *tokei* means watch in Japanese. He wanted the gold watch that my mother had given me for graduation. It was the watch that the Japanese prison personnel could easily have confiscated but didn't. I told him that he could get into trouble for taking my personal belongings from me. All he gave me was a "tough guy" smirk. I demanded to see his commanding officer, but instead, he called a master sergeant to help out.

The master sergeant was obviously put out by my sudden appearance and without even asking who I was barked, "Look, you may speak good English but you're still on the other side." He apparently considered me to be Japanese and not American. He dressed me down for arguing with the sentry.

Again, I demanded to be taken to the commanding officer. By then, I was fuming mad. "Look," I said, "I am a sergeant in the Counterintelligence Corps and I have been a POW all these years after being captured on Corregidor." He was visibly shaken by what I said and he seemed embarassed, but he did not apologize. Reluctantly, he took me to the office of the commanding officer, who was a major.

The major listened to my story and immediately phoned the closest Counter Intelligence Corps (CIC) field office at Bagabac, just outside Manila. As soon as he got off the line, he informed me that the men at the CIC office were astonished to hear that I was alive. The were sending someone over to pick me up. The major ordered his first sergeant to fix me up with a hot shower and a clean set of khakis before the CIC representatives arrived.

The hot shower felt luxurious. After changing into fresh clothes and getting something to eat, I felt like a new man. I was so pumped up with excitement that my illness had subsided. At least the symptoms had.

That afternoon, two lieutenants from the CIC came to pick me up. They greeted me like a long lost brother. It felt good to be back in the fold—again. They drove me back to the CIC field office where they feted me with a party that night. After eating sweet potato leaves and grass for three months, I couldn't resist the food that they placed in front of me. But the mounds of fried chicken, mashed potatoes and gravy, fresh vegetables, real bread and butter, and coffee turned out to be far too rich for my malnourished system. For the next three days, I was very ill. But for the first time in years, being sick did not worry me. There was help within reach and I was free at last—and that's what counted most.

Chapter 12

LOOKING BACK

For me the beginning of the war was much like the end: on both occasions, I was out in the cold. When the war actually broke out, only a handful of people knew where I was. When it ended, no one knew where I was. When I learned the war had ended, I wanted to celebrate, to share my joy and elation. But by the time I finally returned to Manila as a free man, the celebrations had already ended. The bands had stopped playing, the parades had long ended, and there was no more dancing or jubilation in the streets of Manila.

There was still an undercurrent of joy and happiness over the end to the fighting, but the focus was on a return to peace and normalcy. I had anticipated returning to Manila—the beauty and energy of the Pearl of the Orient could uplift the lowest spirits. But all I could see in Manila was a city reduced to rubble. Even the so-called Intramuros, or Walled City, was leveled.

It was time to move on, but it was not easy. The scars of war visible in the city somehow reminded me of the scars on my own body and in my mind. Like the city, I needed to rebuild, redirect my life, and heal physically and mentally.

By the time I got back to CIC headquarters at Bagabac, it was around mid-September. On the very next day, I was ordered to go to the Replacement Depot to get my personnel records back in order. The original records were lost during the hurried retreat from Manila on Christmas Day 1941. On the following day, I should have been given a physical examination. Instead, I was put through a hurried debriefing by CIC agents before being sent immediately to work on the war crimes trials. A CIC account states that I "was one of the few Americans with first-hand knowledge of the events which had transpired in the Japanese-occupied Philippines," and that I was allowed little convalescent time before serving at the trials. Actually, I was given no convalescent time.

Other POWs were hospitalized for two weeks of observation before being sent on convalescent leave, which took place at a hotel of their choice near their home. This leave was intended to provide a gradual reentry into freedom. I received no such leave; I was simply allowed to place a telephone call to my mother. Moreover, the debriefing at CIC headquarters turned into more of an interrogation to determine whether I had been aiding the Japanese instead of the American side. It was disheartening to be treated that way, to have my loyalty questioned after all those years of perilous service. Their denial of privileges but willingness to keep me in service, to me shows a pervasive doubt—a doubt I was helpless to dissuade. I was maddeningly a victim of circumstances.

I was finally reunited with my family in December 1945 during home leave. In September, when the war ended, Colonel Gilbert had told my mother that I was missing in action. When she finally learned that I had survived, she was elated. As much as she wanted to, she could not call me long distance because spoken Japanese was not allowed on such calls.

As I bask in retirement, I look back with gratitude for the gift of life. I came close to losing it. Right now, everything else pales in importance compared to life and the opportunity to make something of it. I survived to serve and give something, however small, back to this country. I did it in the belief that the strength of a democracy depends on giving—particularly of ourselves—not just taking.

Occasionally, I reflect on what I received from my experience. Most noticeably, I suffer from recurring pain from the damage done by the torture. On days when the damp air blows in from the bay area, I suffer pains that require prescription medication. The area around my rotator cuffs feels like a jumble of nerves on fire. My shoulders feel like they are no longer capable of containing my upper arms in their sockets. My back aches regularly, as do my legs, arms, and hands. The pain has plagued me for over fifty years, and doctors say that the pain is something I will have to live with for the rest of my life.

Another legacy of my imprisonment is a firm belief in the strength of willpower. It served me during imprisonment and has maintained me through the years. I live with pain and look to the brighter side of life, no matter how excruciating the pain gets. As when I was younger, I never dawdle and I make it a point to move about as fast as I can. In this way I take my focus off what hurts, making it hurt less thereby. Those around me do not know my restrictions, unless they see the handicapped tag in my car.

The mental trauma and abuse that I endured at the hands of my captors continue, like my aches and pains, to haunt me. For years, and to this very day, I have regarded emotional distress as a sign of weakness. I have never been able to seek professional help. Perhaps it is part of strongly held Buddhist belief in the primacy of mind over matter. Perhaps it came from my Japanese concept of proper behavior. Or perhaps it came from growing up male. Somehow I came to believe that it is shameful to cry or show fear in the face of physical pain or danger. Endurance meant keeping things to oneself. Perhaps my lack of articulation is due also to a tendency of combat veterans to suppress the unbelievably horrifying side of war. Other veterans I know never talk about their experiences except among themselves in the privacy of their clubs or at reunions.

As a member of G2 I was also sworn to secrecy until 1972. And there is the problem of credibility. I often asked myself, "Who would believe my story?" So for years, I have kept everything bottled up inside of me. I kept details of my capture even from my wife. For years, I got up at night shaking, perspiring, and convulsed by latent pangs of trauma and personal demons. I accepted no other way than to cope with the demons by myself. Telling this story has helped me purge some of the the demons that tormented me for years.

181

Although I seem to have garnered few rewards for my service, I remain convinced that the role of intelligence is vital to the security of a democratic society. It is not a line of work for anyone seeking profit or recognition. Success is rarely recognized; only failure is. During World War II, we were a small group, but we were committed. Being part of it taught me something about fulfilling goals that transcended myself in importance. It not only made me a better man, it made me a better citizen.

I came out of the war with a tortured mind. Fortunately, the healing process began early and in an unexpected way.

In February 1947, while stationed in Manila, I was offered a commission by the army, which involved becoming an officer and leaving the enlisted ranks. After giving it some thought, I accepted because I had been in the army since 1941 and I had no idea what my employment prospects would be as a civilian. They ordered me to fly to Tokyo for a preliminary interview. In addition, they asked me to escort a prisoner, a Japanese colonel, back to Tokyo to be sentenced; he had been tried and found guilty by the War Crimes Tribunal in Manila.

The next day, I reported to the airfield and met the colonel. Upon being introduced, the colonel clicked his heels and bowed. I bowed back. He was a man of impressive bearing. His uniform was worn, but he appeared impeccably dressed. He wore winter clothes and carried an overcoat, which I didn't give much thought to at that time. Apparently, he knew what winter was like in Tokyo. I was dressed in my tropicals because the quartermaster office had assured me that I wouldn't need a winter uniform in Tokyo.

He sat next to me, ramrod straight, throughout the long flight to Japan. He was an officer through and through and never once tried to ingratiate himself to me. He asked for nothing and for long stretches, he seemed to be in deep meditation. There was no real conversation between us. But as the trip wore on, I began talking to him. He told me where he had been stationed in the Philippines and some of his battle experiences there. As we talked, I began to see him as a human being like myself and not as an enemy soldier. He made no attempt to plead his case as a soldier. He didn't have to say it—I knew he was doing his duty, just as any good officer would have. It made me think. Not too long ago, we would have been prepared to kill each other on the battlefield and there we were, talking like normal human beings. His fate could very well have been mine.

As we neared Japan, I asked him if he had a family. He said he had a wife and two children; one son and a daughter at home, whom he had not seen in years. As he spoke of his family, a mellowness that had not been in evidence until now began to show in his eyes. It was a look of melancholy and sadness. I asked him where he lived and he replied that he lived in the vicinity of Tokyo but that he had no idea how his family was or what remained of his family home.

I then did something that I would probably not have done under any other circumstances. I offered the colonel one night with his family. I reminded him that Japan was under American occupation and that if he attempted to escape, I would eventually hunt him down no matter where he chose to escape to. He had never expected to see his family again. As he regained his composure, he assured me that he would report wherever I wanted him to. He attempted to bow in gratitude but his seat belt held him in check. He assured me that it was a matter of honor that he face the charges brought against him and that I need not worry about his appearance in the morning.

We landed at Haneda Airport. The fog had rolled in so that it was almost impossible to see anything around us. Everything seemed dark and shrouded in gray. The colonel immediately donned his overcoat and I cursed as the door was opened to let us disembark. I froze as the cold blast of frigid air cut right through my tropical uniform. I had never been so cold in my life.

As we made our way into the terminal, I took the colonel aside and told him to meet me in front of the Meiji Building the following day at 7:30 A.M. He thanked me and I watched as he disappeared into the mist. By then, I was cold but the excitement of being in Japan made me forget about it for awhile. As I made my way through the terminal area, I was struck by the frenetic pace of activity around me. It was a far cry from the languid life of the Philippines. The Japanese employees at the airfield seemed to be in perpetual motion, scurrying around as if there was no tomorrow.

It didn't take long to find my ride to Tokyo. A shuttle bus system had been set up to carry U.S. personnel from Haneda Airport to key areas of downtown Tokyo. The countryside was as bleak as the heavily overcast skies that enveloped us. I was dead tired from the long and virtually sleepless flight from Manila, but I was transfixed by the passing scenery along roads that looked like they had not recovered from the war yet.

As we neared the city, it was obvious that the B-29 bombings had taken a toll. In the outlying areas, the firebombing had leveled just about all of the homes. In many areas, there was only rubble. Ramshackle huts and lean-tos housed the people. The highway that our bus was on seemed like a country road compared to American highways. Occasionally, we came across carts being pushed or pulled by men, women, and children, all dwarfed but undeterred by daunting loads of produce and goods. Our bus often unavoidably crowded them off the road, and in our wake, I saw fear, consternation, and resignation on their faces. It was a look that I had often seen on the faces of people in the Philippines. It was also symptomatic of emotions caused by an overpowering American presence in a foreign land.

There was something to be learned from such incidents. Most of the passengers on the bus felt genuinely sorry for the people who had their loads scattered all over when our bus pushed them off the highway. But there were some GIs who laughed hilariously at such scenes and shouted obscenities at the people from open windows on the bus. I think it was this same kind of crude and boorish behavior that was to become the bane of other well-meaning Western initiatives in Asia. It made me understand why General MacArthur warned against any military occupation of another country beyond a few years.

That night, as the colonel spent his last night with his family, I ate, drank, and smoked to my heart's content. I had American money and felt wealthy and privileged. I was the survivor of a deadly game and I felt as if I were returning from purgatory.

The next morning, I hurried out of the billets to see if the colonel was waiting for me as promised. Our meeting place was the Meiji Building, which is where the war crimes investigation headquarters were located. I was a bit late and as I hurried to the appointed place, I began to worry about whether he would be there.

As I approached the building, I saw him, standing proud and erect. When I got there, he saluted smartly, even though he out-ranked me. He spoke to me in classically polite terms with a choice of words, intonation, and gesture that was beautiful to behold. It was all part of the situational ethics that determines the level of language that is used in interpersonal relations in Japan. He was obviously a well-bred man because he used a high form of the language. He told me how grateful he was to be able to spend one last night with his family. But the dignity and sincerity with which he conveyed his feelings touched me beyond description. He was tough and he exuded every virtue that I had come to associate with a samurai. I truly believe that he was a man capable of committing ritual *hara-kiri* if warranted by circumstances. I kept thinking what a waste of manhood it would be to execute him. Exceptional soldiers are hard to find. Somehow, he seemed completely at peace as he spoke.

After thanking me, he bowed ceremoniously and handed me a token of appreciation from him and his family. It was neatly wrapped in plain paper. Paper was scarce in Japan, but they had used it to wrap my package. I unwrapped it and found two *onigiri*. *Onigiri* are rice balls made by taking a scoop of hot rice and shaping it with both hands.

Rice has been the staff of life in Japan for over two thousand years and it has always been a much valued staple. It symbolizes something that lies at the heart of Japanese culture. The moment I saw the rice balls, I understood what it had meant for him to share them one last time with his family. It was a time of rationing in postwar Japan, and his wife may have sacrificed a family heirloom to get that rice.

Throughout my years of incarceration and torture I never once shed a tear in enduring physical pain. I grew hard in defiance of the brutality inflicted on me by my captors. But, the kindness this man showed in sharing his last supper with me broke through the defenses that had carried me through my horror. I knew what awaited him.

I couldn't suppress the tears. I cried for me and for him. Finally, I was forced to retreat into a quiet corner of the building to regain my composure.

185

The colonel instinctively avoided looking at me. I am sure that he understood my feelings. We were soldiers of differing loyalties and allegiances who had somehow bridged a great divide that had here-tofore existed between us. He was an enemy soldier during the war, but he touched my soul as no one else had ever done. It was just what my tortured soul needed; a return to humanity.

Soon thereafter, the colonel was executed by hanging. Had the war turned out differently, I could very well have been the one being hung.

After my interview with a board of officers, I returned to Manila to await their decision. Soon after, I was commissioned as a lieuten-ant in the U.S. Army and after transferring to the U.S. Air Force, I became a part of the U.S. Occupation Force in Japan.

I spent nineteen years in Japan after the end of the war. During this period, I took the first steps toward trying to live with the pain and anger that still filled me after my traumatic experiences as a POW. When I was being tortured in prison, all I could think of was surviving so I could seek revenge against every one of my tormentors. This rage was still bottled up inside me when the war ended. But once things began to return to normal, this rage began to subside, even though I was still tortured by the traumatic events of the past. I realized this when I encountered my assailants after the war.

During the occupation period, I was chief of the Apprehension and Interrogation Division of the War Crimes Commission, and I had access to all of the POW camps. I located the master sergeant, cap-tain, and major of the Kempeitai who were responsible for the tor-ture I had undergone in the Bilibid Prison. I had them brought to Manila and went to see them, wearing dark glasses to hide my iden-tity. Through an interpreter I asked them, "We are looking for a *nisei* by the name of Sakakida. Did any of you know him?" They each replied in the negative.

I removed my sunglasses and their eyes widened in recognition. They were stupefied and showed no traces of the arrogance I had long associated with them. Looking frightened and guilty, my former torturers prostrated themselves on the ground as if ready to accept any punishment I chose to inflict upon them. But by now I was far too removed from the rage I had felt while in their control; the war was over, and I had no desire to return to bitter hatred and killing. As soldiers in combat we had all done what was required of us. They had done their job, just as I had done mine by escorting the Japanese colonel to his hanging in Tokyo. I was ready to let bygones be bygones. I still don't know where that compassion and forgiveness came from. Wherever they are, I hope that those men have found peace as I have.

Chapter 13

EPILOGUE

The time for reckoning finally arrived in the fall of 1991. The fiftieth anniversary reunion of the Military Intelligence Service was scheduled for 28 October 1991 at the Hyatt Regency Hotel in Monterey, California. I had spent a good part of the year previous to that writing and tinkering with my speech. It was a period of fits and starts, bursts of inspired effort, and writer's block. It had passed quickly and, like many retirees, I felt like I was busier in retirement than I had been before.

One phase of the speech writing was mercifully straightforward. My military records were at least in chronological order. The rest of the trip back into the past was like walking through a Japanese garden. Every juncture produced its own vista and a different set of thoughts and emotions. The Japanese gardeners had it right; life is never a straight line of events.

Ultimately, I had come to feel that I was responsible for my own actions during the war. As trite as that may seem, I learned that there are times when reason alone cannot break into suppressed emotions. People are not like computer software based on logic—they can't be reprogrammed to change their feelings. At some point, I had to involve my own feelings and intuition to breach those bonds and break free. Had I chosen to blame others for my fate, I would probably still be wallowing in remorse, self-pity, and bitter hatred. "What better way to contemplate a blessing," I mused, as I drove along one of the most beautiful stretches of highway in California on the way to Monterey.

The past year had been a time for self-examination and a reassessment of the roots of my heritage. There were myths and realities that I had to sort out for my own good. Myths were a significant part of my early upbringing, but I thought I knew the difference between myth and reality.

My musing led me to wonder whether our parents had pulled the wool over our eyes when they taught us about things like *Yamato damashi*, the mythical "Japanese spirit." I wondered about the tales of filial piety, honesty, loyalty, bravery, and forbearance. "Was all that Japanese propaganda?" I asked myself. I remember many of my friends feeling that way as they grew older and became more Americanized. But when I was imprisoned, those ideas and concepts helped me survive.

As I composed my speech, I began to realize that all the things that I learned through Japanese materials were universal principles necessary to the healthy sustenance of any society, including American society. The *isseis* probably thought so too and that was their contribution to making us better American citizens. Because of that, by the time I became a POW, I knew exactly who I was and what I stood for as an American. Myths were translated into reality allowing us to experience a kind of "American spirit," not unlike the "Japanese spirit" that I had learned about as a child. Without that grounding, it would have been much harder to endure all the torture and humiliation in prison. I discovered that it is possible to have what I can only describe as a spiritual experience at a time of dire need. The price of faith is often steep and painful; just as it should be. That too was impressed on us by the *isseis*, but I didn't believe that either as a child. In spite of my earlier misgivings, those myths formed the basis of my identity and commitment to citizenship.

When the time finally came for me to deliver the speech, I felt I had rehearsed it often enough to be in control, but from the moment of my introduction I was gripped by nervousness. I approached the lectern and I started out very deliberately, but once into it, all traces of nerves disappeared. I had a story to tell and I knew the story better than anyone in the audience. I tried to keep the speech as short as possible but it lasted almost an hour and a half. For all that time, except for the sporadic clatter of dishes, a hushed silence pervaded the huge conference hall. When I was finished, I felt enormously relieved. For good or bad, the story of my experience as a U.S. secret agent and as a POW of the Japanese was finally out. I could begin to close that chapter after fifty years, and it felt good. The war taught me a great deal about the imperfections of the world. In trying to redress some of those imperfections, I sometimes lost perspective and I wondered later why I had done some of the things that I did. One consolation was that I was not reduced to complete cynicism once it was all over.

A long time ago, I heard a story about the pitfalls of cynicism. It seems that a visiting Asian legal scholar at one of our midwestern universities who was an observer at the war crimes trials in Tokyo listened quietly to an intense intellectual debate on the justice meted out at the trials. An Asian-American student who was at the same table asked the scholar what he thought of the heated exchange. He turned to the student and whispered, "In war, justice depends on who wins." When I first heard the story, I had difficulty determining whether the scholar was being realistic or cynical in his remark, but I could understand why he said it.

For many *niseis*, justice was not within easy reach. It had to be earned and the first test was on the battlefield. Reality dictated that the quest be bloody. That is what our parents, many of whom were poor, humble, and uneducated, prepared us for—to rise above ourselves in a struggle for something the law alone could not guarantee. Social acceptance could not be legislated so we had to prove ourselves. In the struggle, tradition, culture, and identity played major roles. They were all important to us at that time.

Yet, it is important to note that neither the cultural heritage that we prided ourselves in, nor our ethnicity were ends in themselves. The end sought was an active involvement in an American culture in which future generations of Japanese-Americans would be allowed to thrive, even if it meant watering down part of our generation's Japanese heritage. What we relied on was not ideology. To be free, we had to look inward before we could reach beyond ourselves.

191

Chapter 14

POSTSCRIPT

On 23 October 1993, at the Capital Reunion of the Military Intelligence Service, held under the auspices of the Japanese-American Veterans Association of Washington, D.C., Richard Sakakida was awarded three medals: the Philippine Defense Medal, the Philippine Liberation Medal, and the National Defense Medal of the Republic of the Philippines.

On 14 April 1994, by order of President Fidel Ramos of the Republic of the Philippines, the Award of the Philippine Legion of Honor, degree of Legionnaire was presented to Richard Sakakida by Ambassador Raul Rabe of the Republic of the Philippines. The ceremony was held at the embassy of the Philippines in Washington, D.C.

General Order 103, issued on that date, cites Richard Sakakida's "exceptionally meritorious conduct in the performance of outstanding service to the Filipino-American freedom fighters as the United States Counterintelligence agent from 22 April 1941 to 20 September 1945." The general order went on to list his achievements and to state that "By those achievements, Mr. Sakakida contributed immeasurably to the liberation of the Philippines, thereby earning for himself, the respect and admiration of the Filipino people."

It is a fitting way to bring this story to a close.

SUGGESTED READINGS

Berry, William A., and James Edwin Alexander. *Prisoner of the Rising Sun*. Norman: University of Oklahoma Press, 1993.

Bunge, Frederick A. M., ed. *Philippines: A Country Study*. Area Handbook Series. Washington, D.C.: Government Printing Office, 1984.

Byas, Hugh. *Government by Assassination*. New York: Alfred A. Knopf, 1942.

Chang, Thelma. *I Can Never Forget, Men of the 100th/442nd*. Honolulu: Sigi Productions Inc., 1991.

Drea, Edward J. *MacArthur's ULTRA: Codebreaking and the War against Japan, 1942–1945*. Lawrence: University Press of Kansas, 1991.

Duus, Masayo Umezawa. *Unlikely Liberators: The Men of the 100th and 442nd*. Honolulu: University of Hawaii Press, 1983.

Edwards, Duval A. *Spy Catchers in the U.S. Army in the War with Japan.*. Gig Harbor, Wash.: Red Apple Publishing, 1994.

Hamm, Diane L., comp. *Military Intelligence: Its Heroes and Legends*. Washington, D.C.: U.S. Government Printing Office, 1987.

Harrington, Joseph. *History of the Defenders of the Philippines, Guam, and Wake Islands, 1941–1945*. Paducah, Ky.: Turner Publishing Company, 1991.

————. *Yankee Samurai: The Secret Role of the Nisei in America's Pacific Victory*. Detroit: Pettigrew Enterprise Ltd., 1979.

Hosokawa, Bill. *Nisei: The Quiet Americans*. New York: William Morrow and Co. Ltd., 1969.

Kennedy, Milly Wood. *Corregidor, Glory, Ghost and Gold*. 1971.

Kerr, E. Bartlett. *Surrender and Survival: The Experience of American POWs in the Pacific, 1941–1945*. New York: William Morrow and Company Inc., 1985.

Kotani, Roland. *The Japanese in Hawaii: A Century of Struggle*. Honolulu: Hawaii Hochi Ltd., 1985.

Morris, Eric. *Corregidor: The End of the Line*. New York: Stein and Day, 1981.

Morton, Louis. *The War in the Pacific: The Fall of the Philippines*. Washington, D.C.: Center of Military History, 1989.

Ogawa, Dennis M. *Kodomo no tame ni: For the Sake of the Children*. Honolulu: University of Hawaii Press, 1983.

Potter, John Deane. *The Life and Death of a Japanese General*. New York: The New American Library, 1962.

Sayer, Ian, and Douglas Botting. *America's Secret Army*. New York: Franklin Watts, 1989.

Talbot, Carol Terry, and Virginia J. Muir. *Escape at Dawn*. Wheaton, Ill.: Tyndale House Publishers, Inc., 1988.

Tsukano, John. *Bridge of Love*. Honolulu: Hawaii Hosts Inc., 1985.

Wainwright, Jonathan M. *General Wainwright's Story*. New York: Bantam Books, 1946.

INDEX

197

ABOUT THE AUTHOR

Wayne S. Kiyosaki was born and raised in Spreckelsville, Maui, Hawaii. Now retired, he worked for the U.S. Department of Defense and the Foreign Broadcast Information Service. During the Korean War, he was commissioned as an officer in the U.S. Air Force. He holds a B.A. from the University of Hawaii, an M.A. from the University of Michigan, and a Ph.D. in political science from the George Washington University in Washington, D.C. He is also the author of *North Korea's Foreign Relations: The Politics of Accommodation, 1945–1975* and *Japanese High-Tech Information: A Beckoning Market*.